NEW DIRECTIONS FOR COMMUNITY COLLEGES

Arthur M. Cohen
EDITOR-IN-CHIEF

Florence B. Brawer
ASSOCIATE EDITOR

Economic and Work Force Development

Geneva Waddell
Montgomery Community College

EDITOR

Number 75, Fall 1991

JOSSEY-BASS INC., PUBLISHERS, San Francisco

MAXWELL MACMILLAN INTERNATIONAL PUBLISHING GROUP
New York • Oxford • Singapore • Sydney • Toronto

EDUCATIONAL RESOURCES INFORMATION CENTER

ERIC Clearinghouse For Junior Colleges

UNIVERSITY OF CALIFORNIA, LOS ANGELES

ECONOMIC AND WORK FORCE DEVELOPMENT
Geneva Waddell (ed.)
New Directions for Community Colleges, no. 75
Volume XIX, number 3
Arthur M. Cohen, Editor-in-Chief
Florence B. Brawer, Associate Editor

Microfilm copies of issues and articles are available in 16mm and 35mm, as well as microfiche in 105mm, through University Microfilms Inc., 300 North Zeeb Road, Ann Arbor, Michigan 48106.

LC 85-644753   ISSN 0194-3081   ISBN 1-55542-767-7

NEW DIRECTIONS FOR COMMUNITY COLLEGES is part of The Jossey-Bass Higher and Adult Education Series and is published quarterly by Jossey-Bass Inc., Publishers, 350 Sansome Street, San Francisco, California 94104-1310 (publication number USPS 121-710) in association with the ERIC Clearinghouse for Junior Colleges. Second-class postage paid at San Francisco, California, and at additional mailing offices. POSTMASTER: Send address changes to New Directions for Community Colleges, Jossey-Bass Inc., Publishers, 350 Sansome Street, San Francisco, California 94104-1310.

SUBSCRIPTIONS for 1991 cost $48.00 for individuals and $70.00 for institutions, agencies, and libraries.

THE MATERIAL in this publication is based on work sponsored wholly or in part by the Office of Educational Research and Improvement, U.S. Department of Education, under contract number RI-88-062002. Its contents do not necessarily reflect the views of the Department, or any other agency of the U.S. Government.

EDITORIAL CORRESPONDENCE should be sent to the Editor-in-Chief, Arthur M. Cohen, at the ERIC Clearinghouse for Junior Colleges, University of California, Los Angeles, California 90024.

Cover photograph by Rene Sheret, Los Angeles, California © 1990.

Printed on acid-free paper in the United States of America.

CONTENTS

PREFACE

The American economy is nourished by a constant stream of new immigrants who are eager to contribute to their new homeland by working hard. While physical stamina and the desire to work were previously the most important employment credentials, today a radically different and evolving world economy requires a revolution in attitudes about what is needed for employment. For example, the technical training required to enter today's highly skilled work force demands that we reframe our assumptions. If the United States is to retain a competitive edge in the global marketplace, technical education must have a vastly altered role.

We are experiencing tremendous technological changes that affect our working and personal lives. We have become aware of the growing economic power of other countries as foreign interests have proliferated in our own country. American business is challenged to maintain a preeminent role in a world economy that is increasingly dependent on technological advancement. Employers are seriously concerned about the increasing difficulty of finding technically skilled employees. National studies regularly report the growing shortage of persons in technical careers. Even the steady increase of salaries has not produced large numbers of entrants into these fields. More fundamental than the lack of employees in these careers, however, is the heightened level of skill and sophistication required to enter and be successful in the present and future work force.

It is clear that our society requires a reexamination of technical training programs in light of the new realities of the marketplace. The truth is that our workplace has rapidly outgrown traditional technical training. The substance of technical education must be improved now. It is critical that specific steps be taken to broaden and enrich the training offered by our educational institutions.

The first and most essential step is a joint institutional and public commitment to a fresh interpretation of the nature of technical education. We need to expand our concept of training to encompass not only the acquisition of skills but also the development of the whole person. At the same time, curricula and programs must be reevaluated and revised to provide the broad general background needed to achieve these goals. Finally, partnerships must be developed between industry and education to obtain the sources and support required for the task of reframing technical training within the context of higher education.

Nothing short of revolutionary thinking will create the programs we need. Employers have been clear in defining the skills that they require from employees. Now educators need to reassess their natural conservatism and become the catalysts of change. It is time to join the forces of the private and public sectors and provide students with the education required to accommodate the profound and inevitable social and economic transformations of the twenty-first century.

This issue of *New Directions for Community Colleges* reinforces the concept of skills training and development of the whole person. The focus is on meeting economic and work force development needs in local communities within a global economy.

Robert E. Parilla

Robert E. Parilla is president of Montgomery College in Montgomery County, Maryland.

EDITOR'S NOTES

Urgent attention must be given to meeting the economic and work force development needs of America. A snapshot of the work force in many American communities reveals countless areas where further training and retraining are imperative. For example, rapid technological advances are changing the character of health care services, which in turn is changing expectations of health care workers. Changes such as the growing complexity of jobs, declining numbers of entry-level employees, and organizational restructuring have implications for both economic and work force development.

According to Anthony Carnevale of the American Society for Training and Development, employers spend at least $30 billion on formal training and $180 billion on informal, on-the-job training each year (Carnevale, Gainer, and Villet, 1990). Research suggests that learning in school and on the job is the most important factor in American economic growth and productivity. Research also shows that human resource efforts account for two-thirds of the nation's productivity since 1929 and that workers must be highly skilled for productivity to remain at a high level.

It is particularly difficult to focus on economic and work force development since the target is rapidly changing. For example, several forces are reshaping the work force and the nature of work, including increasing work force diversity, competing demands of work and family, global competition, the growing importance of strategic human resource planning, the need to reeducate employees for new technologies and more demanding jobs, and renewed interest in ethics and social responsibility (Coates, Jarratt, and Mahaffie, 1990).

Many community colleges have experienced great success in contributing to economic and work force development by utilizing their strengths of program flexibility, diversity, adaptability, and responsiveness to societal needs. As the contributors to this volume, *Economic and Work Force Development,* indicate, opportunities for innovations and renovations are plentiful in community colleges. The authors were chosen because of their practical experience, expertise, and diversity of perceptions. Interwoven among the trends, innovations, problems, and solutions that they consider are the following recommendations:

1. Reframe technical education programs to focus on the development of the whole person.
2. Develop partnerships between industry and education to obtain resources and support.
3. Formalize new priorities, roles, and partnerships for strategic alignment with state economic policies.

3

4. Consider the advantages of a technical-preparatory track to prepare high school students for technical careers not requiring a degree.
5. Identify advantages and disadvantages of hosting a Small Business Development Center.
6. Develop business incubators to promote the formation of new businesses.
7. Enhance existing programs to meet specific health care industry and community needs, seeking support from credentialing and accrediting agencies.
8. Strengthen cooperative education opportunities by working with local unemployment and social service agencies and by providing basic skills training.
9. Consider providing employment and life-skills training through pre-cooperative education work experience.
10. Assist in improving work place literacy by strengthening partnerships with public school systems.
11. Form partnerships with local employment and social service agencies to recruit at-risk students into programs that include work experience.
12. Develop a regional nonprofit economic development organization to promote regional economic development as needed.
13. Expand distance learning opportunities, carefully examining new technology and its applicability versus complexity.
14. Export the American community college concept to interested countries and consider importing ideas from other countries to improve our system.
15. Expand our global vision so that our potential arena in which to sell, train, and create working relationships will grow.
16. Remove self-imposed obstacles such as inadequate international education and experience that diminish our ability to participate in the worldwide marketplace.
17. Recruit advisory boards composed of corporate executives willing to devote time and resources to international education.
18. Provide or improve training for individuals dealing with day-to-day export operations.
19. Use evaluation results to demonstrate the costs and benefits of economic and work force development to campus and community groups.

In *Innovation in the Community College,* Terry O'Banion contends that "the community college rode the crest of the wave of expanding opportunity in a society determined to establish a new order of justice, equality, and economic prosperity. In more recent years it has become a force that pushes the wave of expanded opportunity instead of riding it" (1989, p. 2).

Geneva Waddell
Editor

References

Carnevale, A. P., Gainer, L. J., and Villet, J. *Training in America: The Organization and Strategic Role of Training.* San Francisco: Jossey-Bass, 1990.

Coates, J. F., Jarratt, J., and Mahaffie, J. B. *Future Work: Seven Critical Forces Reshaping Work and the Work Force in North America.* San Francisco: Jossey-Bass, 1990.

O'Banion, T. (ed.). *Innovation in the Community College.* New York: American Council on Education/Macmillan, 1989.

Geneva Waddell is associate staff and adjunct professor at Montgomery Community College, Montgomery County, Maryland.

The 1990s will become the decade of strategic alignment of community colleges and state economic development policy— a formalization of new priorities, roles, and partnerships.

Strategic Alignment of Community Colleges and State Economic Policy

John G. Melville, Thomas J. Chmura

Emerging from a period of irreversible economic change in the 1980s, the United States now must confront a new global reality. This change has already ushered in a new activism and a new focus in state economic development policy (Committee for Economic Development, 1986; National Governors' Association, 1987; Fosler, 1988; Osborne, 1988).

The rules for success in economic development have changed from low-cost labor, land, and taxes to high-quality investment in human resources, research and development, and other elements of economic infrastructure (SRI International, 1987). The 1980s brought a flood of new state initiatives, many specifically aimed at enhancing or better tapping the resources of community colleges for economic development.

In the 1990s, however, more is needed than pilot initiatives and special programs linking state economic policy and community colleges. Although experimentation must continue, we must use what we have learned over the past decade to institute more far-reaching changes.

The 1980s: A Decade of Necessary Experimentation

Recognizing the importance of skilled and adaptable workers to high value-added economic development, state policymakers in the 1980s looked increasingly to their community colleges for help in implementing new directions in state economic policy. Community colleges were uniquely equipped to upgrade the skills of the work force through education and training.

As the focus began to shift to community colleges as economic development partners, however, other roles were explored as well. Community colleges turned out to be excellent sources of management and technical assistance for new, small businesses. Also, they were well positioned to provide basic technology transfer services to existing businesses. And, they could provide information and insights useful in the development of business attraction strategies.

The most common approach at the state level was to create new programs that made special monies available outside the traditional, higher education funding process. This approach enabled state policymakers to earmark funds for specific economic development purposes. And it enabled community colleges to play a more direct role in state economic development while enhancing the quality of their educational programs—all without substantially interfering with their traditional missions.

During the 1980s, many states used this approach both to tap the resources of their community colleges and to avoid the more difficult challenge of restructuring the missions of these institutions. However, some states went beyond pilot programs and took steps that have fundamentally changed the roles and mission of their community colleges in economic development. These states have begun the process of "strategic alignment" of their community colleges with economic development policy. The success of their pioneering efforts provides encouragement for other states in helping community colleges to make major changes as needed.

Oregon: Taking Responsibility for Small Business Assistance

Building on a successful pilot program at Lane Community College in Eugene, Oregon, the state created a new network of Small Business Development Centers in 1983. Every community college in Oregon was given the responsibility of serving the needs of small businesses in their service areas. This structural change allowed the colleges to combine their own resources with special state monies and federal funds to pursue their new mission. As a result, Oregon's community colleges have become the statewide delivery mechanism and coordinators of programs for small business and entrepreneurial assistance.

The network is centrally coordinated through a state office at Lane Community College because of the college's long experience in small business assistance. This office provides technical assistance to community colleges across the state in providing a host of small business assistance services. As the state has sought to diversify its economy from a traditional commodity agriculture and forest products base, the centers have developed an international trade program that analyzes product trade potentials and marketing plans, produces workbooks on financing and international business plans, and organizes conferences on topics such as competing for federal research and development funds.

Initial evaluations of the network have shown excellent results. In one year, the centers were critical to the creation of 218 new businesses. An additional 150 firms expanded their sales, and 300 companies developed comprehensive business plans and marketing and advertising strategies for the first time. Counseling services increased the number of employees in client firms an average of 41 percent for part-time and 54 percent for full-time personnel.

Most important, the network has triggered a fundamental restructuring within the state's community colleges. New state and federal funds have been matched by local institutional funds at an average of better than one to one, and in some cases as high as nine to one. Oregon's community colleges have capitalized on the opportunity not only to tap new state and federal funds but also to refocus internal resources on a critical state need. In the process of subsuming small business assistance into their missions, these institutions have not compromised their traditional roles. In fact, their teaching and public service missions have taken on new dimensions appropriate to the changing demands of the marketplace (SRI International, 1987; McNett, 1987).

Arizona: Actively Anticipating Community Needs

In the 1980s, Arizona sought to change the nature of the community college relationship to its service area. In many of the state's community colleges, a more active service orientation has been forged. Rather than simply react to requests for assistance, institutions are now beginning to anticipate economic development needs and actively create demand for their services.

Community colleges are actively serving the state's small business sector through a network of centers much like those in Oregon. One college has established a farm business management program to actively reach out to a group that is key to the economic vitality of its service area. Another college is producing a weekly radio show and offering "wellness checkups" and brief evaluations of the competitiveness of small firms.

The Maricopa Community College District in metropolitan Phoenix has encouraged its institutions to participate at the front end of their region's economic development efforts. Colleges work closely with local economic development organizations to produce promotional literature on customized work force recruitment and training services available to prospective new firms and existing expanding firms.

In each of these cases, Arizona's community colleges have formalized a new, active partnership with industry and economic development organizations. This contrasts with traditional approaches in which community colleges have been seen as followers—receptive to requests for assistance but reliant on others for guidance in the economic development arena (SRI International, 1987).

Illinois: Building a Foundation and Rewarding Innovation

Hurt by recession in the early 1980s, Illinois looked to its community colleges for more direct economic development help than ever before sought. The state devised an approach that can serve as a model for the 1990s. At a minimum, the new approach required a shift of priorities in every community college district in the state, but it also actively encouraged and amply rewarded the most entrepreneurial community colleges in economic development.

The Illinois Economic Development Grant Program was established in 1982 to provide incentive funding to the state's community colleges. Operated by the Illinois Community College Board and funded through a legislative appropriation of over $3 million, the program distributes grants of various sizes to colleges across the state. The minimum requirement for each grant is that the college must formally establish an office of economic development with an executive director to coordinate activities. Some adhere to this minimum, but as the years have passed most colleges in the state now have additional staff members supporting their economic development directors.

Grants have ranged from less than $50,000 to more than $350,000, helping fund a broad range of economic development services and projects such as customized training for business, entrepreneurship training and assistance, and technical assistance to local economic development groups regarding industrial recruitment strategies. Some of the more advanced colleges and districts have established business incubators and technology transfer programs. While a minimum standard is required, the range of possible economic development services and projects is not limited. Instead, the state's community colleges are actively encouraged to devise new services that meet the specific needs of their regions.

By establishing a minimum standard and then making incentive funds available for innovation, Illinois has in less than a decade created an unprecedented shift toward economic development among its community colleges. It has simultaneously rewarded the brightest stars for their institutional entrepreneurship and brought along those colleges with little experience in economic development.

A key element of the program is the commitment to professional development of college economic development staff. Realizing that not all college personnel are equally familiar with new kinds of college-business interaction, the Illinois Community College Board provides seminars, conferences, and a newsletter to share experiences and help local staff learn new techniques (SRI International, 1987; Powers, Powers, Betz, and Aslanian, 1988).

Ohio: Making Technology Transfer a Community College Priority

Ohio has attempted to make its community colleges part of a multifaceted state technology development and transfer strategy—a critical dimension of economic development. The state established the Thomas Edison Program, a comprehensive effort that has produced a seed development fund and advanced technology centers and incubators across the state. Like several other states (for example, Pennsylvania, New York, and Massachusetts), Ohio's technology development and transfer strategy is centered on the research-based colleges and universities of the state. However, more so than in any other state, Ohio's strategy requires that community colleges play a critical role.

To date, eight Edison Technology Centers have been funded, with community colleges acting as technology transfer agents. Two centers are particularly noteworthy: those at the Lorain County and Cuyahoga County Community Colleges. At Lorain, a center was created to help local manufacturers become familiar with new technological equipment in areas such as robotics, computer-integrated manufacturing, microelectronics, and computer-aided design and manufacturing. The center has received numerous equipment donations in return for its indirect "marketing" of new technology products to local businesses. With the latest technological equipment on hand, the college is able not only to serve the economic development needs of local industry but also to make its students and faculty the most technologically current (and valuable) human resources in the region.

Cuyahoga has made its mark by offering some of the best, most up-to-date multitechnological training in that region. The college, through its center, acquires and adapts customized education and training packages in specific, advanced fields of technology. Through annual manufacturing surveys, it also actively seeks to determine the level of technology use in its service area, the need for adoption of new technology, and the need for working training and retraining.

In addition to technology centers, Ohio has instituted other structural changes to enable community colleges to play a greater role in technology transfer. The Ohio Technology Transfer Organization was created as a network of state technology transfer agents (not unlike traditional agricultural extension agents) who work with local industry. Operated in collaboration with Ohio State University, the program has agents at community and technical colleges across the state. A Productivity Improvement Challenge Program was also created to help community colleges follow through with local businesses in need of assistance by underwriting customized training activities (American Association of Community and Junior Colleges, 1987; McNett, 1987).

South Carolina: Investing in Comprehensive Flexibility

South Carolina has developed a system of technical education and training that is intended to be especially sensitive to the changing skill needs of business. The state's approach has three components: (1) Special Schools train workers for specific jobs in specific companies, similar to customized training programs in other states. (2) Technical Education Center (TEC) colleges offer a wide variety of technical degree programs, much like technical and community colleges offer in other states. And (3) resource centers focus on specific technologies or industries, helping upgrade both college faculty and industry employees in the latest developments in specific fields.

The uniqueness of South Carolina's approach is that each component has long been considered essential to the state's economic competitiveness. The state's technical education system was established in 1961 as an economic development program to build a skilled labor pool and thereby attract new companies and encourage the expansion of existing companies. The program began with Special Schools and TECs, with the TECs later becoming fully accredited colleges. After determining the need to keep pace with increasingly rapid technological change, the state added resource centers at select TEC colleges.

South Carolina has established a system that addresses education and training needs at three levels: immediate customized training, longer-term generic education, and lifelong learning. The Special Schools meet the first set of needs, working with company management to tailor training and provide short, intensive instruction.

The TEC colleges are set up to conduct longer-term education and training programs, with generally more flexibility and faster start-up and shutdown than demonstrated by their counterparts in other states. Close communication with industry has produced exceptional results: Recent statistics gathered by the colleges indicate that approximately 85 percent of graduates of technical programs are placed in jobs related to their training.

The resource centers represent the state's recognition of ongoing changes in technical fields that are important to the economic competitiveness of local industry and the economic well-being of individuals. The centers focus on such areas as office automation, advanced machine tooling, microelectronics, computer applications, robotics, water quality, electromechanical maintenance, and tourism. In each area, the center serves as a focal point to attract local and national technology and industry experts (SRI International, 1987; Powers, Powers, Betz, and Aslanian, 1988).

North Carolina: Creating the Climate for Collaboration

What characterizes North Carolina is a recognition that special attention, resources, and people are needed to make the contacts and to schedule the time necessary for community colleges to develop partnerships with the outside world. More than almost any other state, North Carolina actively invests in people and structures and facilitates connections between community colleges and industry, and between community colleges and economic development organizations and agencies.

At every level, the state has created mechanisms to follow through on collaboration opportunities. At the highest level, the North Carolina Board of State Community Colleges has an Industrial Services Division, which administers short-term training programs and works closely with the state Department of Commerce to assemble attractive recruitment packages for economic development prospects. The division oversees North Carolina's New and Expanding Industries Program in cooperation with local and state offices of the Industrial Developers Association, the state Department of Commerce, local chambers of commerce, and other industrial groups. It maintains regional managers to match individual firms and community colleges in customized training partnerships.

At the local community college level, the state is also committed to providing the means necessary for building partnerships. It provides targeted monies for Cooperative Skills Training Centers to institutionalize close working relationships with local industry. In addition, the state provides funds to local institutions to pay the salaries of instructors for up to two months per year of educational or industry leave for professional development (SRI International, 1987; McNett, 1987).

California: Using Intermediary Organizations as Catalysts

Unlike other states, California not only has looked to existing and new intermediary organizations in regions across the state to bring industry and community colleges closer together, but also, in the 1980s, the state chose not to put community colleges at or near the core of its economic development strategy. California's strategy is mostly laissez-faire. Many individual colleges became much more active on their own in economic development, especially in providing contract training for specific firms, while other colleges did little. The major, noteworthy departure from this strategy is California's unique use of intermediary organizations as outside catalysts for change.

Perhaps the most striking example of this approach is the Technology Exchange Center (TEC [to be distinguished from South Carolina's Technical Education Center]). Located in Orange County, TEC is a nonprofit corporation founded by a coalition of over two hundred leaders in local business, education, government, and labor. TEC operates through a cadre of field representatives that find businesses interested in or trying to implement a new technology but without the staff time, resources, or expertise to train their employees sufficiently. The center matches these companies with a community college or other training organization that can incorporate the desired technology into its curriculum and, if necessary, help locate people to be trained.

The concept for the center was developed in the early 1980s in response to a growing need for work force upgrading in the region. TEC became a reality in 1982 with the help of a major contract from California's Employment Development Department to pay staffing costs. In less than three years, TEC became totally self-supporting, relying solely on fees for service from local colleges and businesses (SRI International, 1987; Roe, 1989).

Another example of seeding an intermediary organization to encourage community college and industry collaboration is found in the San Francisco Bay Area. A regional business group, the Bay Area Council, has undertaken several activities with state encouragement. With funding from the California Community Colleges Chancellor's Office, the Bay Area Council has developed and disseminated two guidebooks: one for community colleges on how to work with business and one for business on how to access local colleges (SRI International, 1988a, 1988b).

The Bay Area Council also acts as a broker for California's Employment Training Panel, the state's innovative retraining and skills-upgrading program. The council helps individual firms prepare funding applications and locate third-party trainers, including community colleges. In return for playing this intermediary role, the council receives a small commission.

The 1990s: A Decade of Strategic Alignment

As illustrated in this chapter, several states began the 1990s well on their way toward strategic alignment of their community colleges with economic development policy. However, for every promising sign of strategic alignment, there are many more states that are still in the process of experimentation. Although most have established pilot initiatives to link community colleges to state economic policy, few have pushed beyond this first stage.

To meet the challenges of the 1990s, small-scale programs will simply not be enough. We must look to the leaders: states that have proven that more comprehensive changes can be made and can produce substantial payoffs for all parties concerned. The evidence is clear: Major investments and structural changes at the community college level have resulted in both major economic development benefits and stronger colleges in several states. This fact can embolden other states that are still experimenting and are unsure about moving ahead in a more proactive manner.

In conclusion, leading states have shown us the following: (1) New community college missions can be introduced quickly and effectively and naturally build off existing strengths, as Illinois, Oregon, and Ohio have demonstrated in the areas of economic development, small business assistance, and technology transfer. (2) Strong commitment to flexibility can create a climate of active and innovative service, as Arizona and South Carolina have found at the grassroots and statewide levels. And (3) new investments in "collaboration brokers" can produce a multitude of benefits that far exceed their costs, as North Carolina and California have discovered inside and outside their community colleges.

Building off the experience of the leading innovators of the 1980s, every region of the country should be able to move more quickly and effectively toward strategic alignment of community colleges and state economic policy in the 1990s. In light of the rapid progress that many states have made in the last decade, this goal is not unrealistic. In fact, our foreign competitors may not allow us the luxury of waiting any longer.

References

American Association of Community and Junior Colleges. *The Role of Community, Technical, and Junior Colleges in Technical Education/Training and Economic Development: A National Forum.* Washington, D.C.: American Association of Community and Junior Colleges, 1987. 79 pp. (ED 312 000)

Committee for Economic Development. *Leadership for Dynamic State Economies.* Washington, D.C.: Committee for Economic Development, 1986.

Fosler, F. S. (ed.). *The New Economic Role of American States.* New York: Oxford University Press, 1988.

McNett, I. *The Development Triangle: Community College Assistance for Economic Growth.* Washington, D.C.: Northeast-Midwest Institute, Center for Regional Policy, 1987. 41 pp. (ED 289 528)

National Governors' Association. *Jobs, Growth, and Competitiveness: Productive People, Productive Policies.* Washington, D.C.: National Governors' Association, 1987. 107 pp. (ED 290 350)

Osborne, D. *Laboratories of Democracy.* Boston: Harvard Business School Press, 1988.

Powers, D. R., Powers, M. F., Betz, F., and Aslanian, C. B. *Higher Education in Partnership with Industry: Opportunities and Strategies for Training, Research, and Economic Development.* San Francisco: Jossey-Bass, 1988.

Roe, M. A. *Education and U.S. Competitiveness: The Community College Role.* Austin: IC2 Institute, University of Texas, 1989.

SRI International. *Building Education and Training into State Economic Development Strategy: Options for Hawaii Executive and Legislative Action.* Menlo Park, Calif.: SRI International, 1987.

SRI International. *A Community College Guide to Working with Employers in the Bay Area.* Menlo Park, Calif.: SRI International, 1988a.

SRI International. *An Employers' Guide to Working with Community Colleges in the Bay Area.* Menlo Park, Calif.: SRI International, 1988b.

John G. Melville is senior policy analyst at the Center for Economic Competitiveness, SRI International, Menlo Park, California.

Thomas J. Chmura is deputy director of the Greater Baltimore Committee, Baltimore, Maryland.

As state leaders look for ways to incorporate the concept of human capital into their official policy making, why should community colleges be part of the response?

Investing in Human Capital: State Strategies for Economic Development

Lawrence A. Nespoli

Emerging throughout the United States is a new federalism. As a result, states are playing a more active role than is the federal government in setting public policy. This chapter examines recent initiatives of state governments and boards in developing economic development policy and describes how community colleges are becoming active partners in these efforts.

Recognizing that the value of human resources in economic development is overlooked frequently, this chapter addresses this imbalance by placing the policy discussion about economic development within the framework of human capital. The discussion starts with the assumption that education and training are the primary systems for investing in human capital.

Although only recently formulated in economic theory, the concept of human capital is now accepted by experts in growth economics, and the contribution of human capital to economic growth is recognized as greater than that of physical capital. However, the concept of human capital, the philosophy behind it, and the role of community colleges in investing in it have not yet been fully embraced and implemented by public policymakers throughout the states.

Why Community Colleges?

As state leaders look for ways to incorporate the concept of human capital into their official policy-making, why should community colleges be part of the response? The answer relates directly to what human capital is and how it can be further developed.

NEW DIRECTIONS FOR COMMUNITY COLLEGES, no. 75, Fall 1991 © Jossey-Bass Inc., Publishers

17

Simply stated, human capital is people potential. For the people potential needed to fuel our states' economies, there are only two sources: new entrants to the work force and the current work force.

It has been widely reported that most of the new entrants to the American work force between now and the year 2000 will be individuals from disadvantaged backgrounds (Johnston, 1987; Hudson Institute, 1988; Hodgkinson, 1985). More specifically, women, minorities, and immigrants will account for over 80 percent of the net additions to the American labor force over this period of time. These populations will clearly need special services and assistance if they are to succeed in the workplace. As open-door institutions that have historically served disadvantaged students, community colleges have the expertise and the commitment to provide the kind of special attention that these new workers will need.

But no matter how well we educate and train new entrants to the work force, that effort alone will not be enough. Eighty percent of the people that will be working in the year 2000 are working now. Thus, increases in the productivity of the current work force must also be a top priority. These workers are, by definition, part-time, adult learners—the very students that community colleges have served so well for the past three decades. No other organizations are more ready or capable than community colleges to respond to the training needs of the nontraditional "students" that comprise the current work force.

In short, to the statements of those state leaders who recognize that people are our greatest resource, it can be added that community colleges are our greatest resource for helping people to achieve their fullest potential. This is true for people seeking to enter the work force as well as for those already employed.

State Role in Building Human Capital

State government is where the action will be in the 1990s on a wide range of public policy issues. Thus, the question is not whether states should be involved in setting economic development policy but rather how they should be involved. And given the potential role for community colleges noted above, the more important question concerns the proper role of state government vis-à-vis local community colleges throughout the state.

To a considerable extent, the relationship between state governments and community colleges flows from the level of financial support that states make available to the colleges. As the level of state support increases, one can generally expect a more active role by the states in community college affairs. This is neither all good nor all bad.

The states have in fact increased their support for community colleges over the past decades in relation to the support from local government. In 1958, over 40 percent of total operating revenues for community colleges came from local government sources (Breneman and Nelson, 1981). That figure has now decreased to about 10 percent as almost all states have moved into the position of funding the largest portion of community college budgets (Tillery and Wattenbarger, 1985).

State power has likewise increased (Tillery and Wattenbarger, 1985). How the states choose to exercise this power will go a long way in determining the ability of community colleges to effectively build human capital for the state and national economies. Centralized state control of community colleges, for example, could seriously compromise the community college role in economic development policy.

This assessment is not designed to minimize the critical role that the states must play. As Newman (1987) points out, the state and federal governments have been the catalysts for the major changes in American higher education, including the land-grant movement, the increased access of minorities and women, and the current concern for economic development. Newman concludes, "A successful system . . . depends not on the choices of either centralization or decentralization. Rather, it depends on centralizing (and decentralizing) the right things. The day-to-day management of academic programs, including appointments and promotions, the development of the curriculum, and the management of campus life belong at the campus level. The establishment of system priorities . . . and the creation of fiscal controls are central functions" (p. 57). This combination of centralized planning and coordination with decentralized management is especially critical when forging state economic development policies. The free-market principles at work in the state economies require flexible, hands-on decision making that only campus administrators can provide.

Overall, state government should rely less on its regulatory powers and more on positive financial incentives to encourage college improvement and effectiveness (National Governors' Association, 1986). This approach will serve the states well as their community colleges seek to build human capital through technical training programs, and physical capital through technology transfer programs.

Building Human Capital Through Technical Training

America needs more technical training. Our postsecondary education system has traditionally been strong in producing professionals, scientists, and managers but weaker at preparing technicians who work at the point of production or service. This imbalance has led to an economic profile that makes us good at invention but less effective at getting products into the marketplace (Carnevale and Schultz, 1988). Certainly we need Ph.D. scientists and engineers to design new products; but we also need trained technicians to build, test, and sell these products and repair them when they break (Tschechtelin, 1988).

By investing in technical training, states can build the specific human capital that is so critically needed in today's economy. This means technical training for new entrants to the work force and for the current work force.

Most new entrants to the work force are recent high school graduates or those who never finish school. Three out of four of these young people will probably never earn a baccalaureate degree (W. T. Grant Foundation, 1988). How can we make winners out of these students? Helping them is the right thing to do, and it is sound economic development policy as well. We will have little human capital to waste in the coming decade (American Association of Community and Junior Colleges, 1984).

Part of the answer is that educators should stop setting the bachelor's degree as the one and only goal for all students and start emphasizing two-year and even one-year programs that provide an entry into important career paths. Fifteen of the twenty fastest growing occupations in the 1990s will require some college, but less than a four-year degree (Johnston, 1987). Individuals trained as legal assistants, nurses, and computer-aided design and manufacturing technicians will be in great demand. Why, then, do many parents continue to encourage their sons and daughters to become doctors, lawyers, and engineers—sometimes to the exclusion of other career possibilities? Obviously, the answer has something to do with the considerable prestige of the professions, and the incomes associated with them. But the preference is also partly a result of educators who are not doing a good job of promoting technical training programs and showing their connection to fulfilling, well-paying jobs and careers.

The "2 + 2" programs being developed by community colleges throughout the country are an important step in the right direction (Parnell, 1985). These programs connect the junior and senior years of high school with the first two years of college through a structured and closely coordinated curriculum. Students can then see the whole picture, the clear purpose of their studies. All high schools have college-preparatory tracks; they should similarly have "2 + 2" technical-preparatory tracks pointing to careers in technical fields that do not require four years of college.

One of the administrative strengths of "2 + 2" programs for technical training is that they can be pursued by community colleges and local schools in a decentralized manner (Waddell, 1990). To the extent that states need to be involved at all—perhaps to encourage development of the "2 + 2" concept where it has not yet taken hold—state government and state boards might consider categorical grants to support initiatives in this area.

In responding to the needs of current workers, states tend to take a more active role. They have at their disposal a variety of training and placement programs, some federally sponsored and some supported entirely by state resources. Through these programs, states are able to serve as brokers between colleges and business leaders and to provide funding for needed training. A number of successful state programs designed to increase the productivity of current workers through technical training are described below. While all types of institutions are eligible to participate, community colleges have been an especially important partner with state government in these and similar programs over the past twenty years.

California: Employment Training Panel. This program was established in 1983 to prepare workers for the structural changes taking place in California's economy. The panel contracts with schools or employers to set up training programs that are performance-based. The training is funded by a special .1 percent tax levied on employers in addition to their regular unemployment insurance taxes. The philosophy of the program is that job training can prevent unemployment and increase business productivity. The first long-term follow-up study of the program, completed in 1986, found that wages increased 55 percent after training, and unemployment decreased 63 percent (National Governors' Association, 1987).

Florida: Sunshine State Skills Corporation. Started by the Florida legislature in 1985, this program places the responsibility for training and retraining employees directly on community colleges. It reflects the commitment and policy within Florida to focus on community colleges as the chief resource for stimulating economic development. Grants are made by the State Board for Community Colleges to support training programs by community colleges for new, expanding, or diversifying businesses. The business partners must match the grants dollar for dollar. In 1986, cash and in-kind contributions from businesses totaled $2,253,048. State funding for the program was $700,000 in the first year, $700,000 again in the second year, and $3 million in the third year (Magruder, 1988).

Iowa: Industrial New Jobs Training Program. This program uses a creative financing mechanism to pay for customized training provided by the state's fifteen community colleges. Tax-exempt training certificates are issued by the colleges and sold in the financial markets to pay for the up-front costs of the training. Repayment of the certificates is made, normally over ten years, through a withholding tax of 1.5 percent of the wages of the new jobs that are created and through a portion of the property taxes on new facilities and equipment (National Governors' Association, 1987; Waddell, 1990).

Maryland: Partnership Through Workforce Quality. The purpose of this program is to improve the competitive position of Maryland businesses by upgrading the skills and productivity of current workers. Two basic kinds of services are offered. The Department of Economic and Employment Development provides business assistance services to help businesses assess their training needs and then develop training plans. The second type of service is through incentive grants to assist businesses in actually obtaining the customized training that they require. The grants pay up to half the cost of the training programs; employers pay the other half. Training is provided primarily by Maryland's seventeen community colleges. In

1989, $1 million was appropriated for the partnership program (Waddell, 1990).

Massachusetts: Bay State Skills Corporation. This quasi-public, state-funded organization was established in 1981 to increase the supply of skilled workers in Massachusetts. The corporation provides 50 percent of the funding, with the other 50 percent provided by participating businesses and industry. Colleges are used as contractors to provide the training that is required. Over six hundred companies and one hundred colleges have participated in the program. The Bay State program has served as a model for other states seeking to build public-private partnerships through which current workers can receive the training that they need (Charner, 1986).

Building Physical Capital Through Technology Transfer

While not the focus of this chapter, it should be noted that community colleges can also make significant contributions to physical capital development, principally through technology transfer programs. Technology transfer means the application of new technological breakthroughs to the physical workplace, to the "factory floor." New technologies cannot have a significant impact on economic development until successful technology transfer occurs.

Community colleges can help transfer new technologies into the workplace in several ways. They can, for example, serve as information clearinghouses on new technologies, they can help firms make wise investments in new physical capital by providing demonstrations of new technologies, and they can support prototype-production processes so that companies can test new technologies without halting production (Breuder, 1988).

Many states are putting community colleges to work in precisely these ways. The Ohio Technology Transfer Organization, for example, operates through that state's twenty-four community colleges in cooperation with Ohio State University. The network is supported by full-time technology agents on each community college campus who provide technology information and technical assistance to businessmen throughout the state. Similarly, Maryland's Office of Technology is working with the University of Maryland to stimulate the development of new technologies, and with community colleges to ensure the successful application of these technologies throughout the state's economy.

Conclusion

Noted educator and philosopher John Gardner once observed that community colleges are the "greatest American educational invention of the twentieth century" (Gardner, 1968). While Gardner's statement may be true for a number of reasons, the "invention" that we call community colleges is making its greatest contribution by carrying out state economic development policies and initiatives. More specifically, community colleges are the best vehicle available to the states for investing in human capital.

Economists, while historically slow to embrace the concept of human capital, now recognize the importance of investing in it, along with investment in physical capital, in order to sustain long-term economic growth. Most typically, this means building human capital through education and technical training programs.

For new entrants to the work force in the 1990s, many of whom will be from minority and disadvantaged backgrounds, community colleges offer the special services and assistance that will be needed to succeed. For current workers seeking to improve their job skills, community colleges offer a long track record of successful, continuing education programs for the adult learner. And for corporate leaders looking to upgrade their physical plants, community colleges can provide needed assistance through technology transfer initiatives.

The role of the states in these efforts should entail strong leadership through statewide planning and coordination, along with incentive-funding programs where appropriate. Responsibility for the delivery of programs, however, must remain at the local campus level. As the Soviet Union and most of the Eastern Bloc countries are now recognizing the limitations of their highly centralized economies, it would be ironic indeed if community colleges, "the greatest American invention of the twentieth century," were to move in the opposite direction.

References

American Association of Community and Junior Colleges. *Putting America Back to Work: The Kellogg Leadership Initiative.* Washington, D.C.: American Association of Community and Junior Colleges, 1984. 66 pp. (ED 245 738)

Breneman, D. W., and Nelson, S. C. *Financing Community Colleges: An Economic Perspective.* Washington, D.C.: Brookings Institution, 1981.

Breuder, R. L. "Technology Transfer and Training: The Critical Challenge." *Community, Technical, and Junior College Journal,* 1988, 59 (2), 30–33.

Carnevale, A. P., and Schulz, E. R. "Technical Training in America: How Much and Who Gets It?" *Training and Development Journal,* 1988, 42 (11), 18–32.

Charner, I. *Higher Education and the State: New Linkages for Economic Development.* Washington, D.C.: National Institute for Work and Learning, 1986.

Gardner, J. W. *No Easy Victories.* New York: Harper & Row, 1968.

Hodgkinson, H. L. *All One System: Demographics of Education: Kindergarten Through Graduate School.* Washington, D.C.: Institute for Educational Leadership, 1985.

Hudson Institute. *Opportunity 2000.* Washington, D.C.: Government Printing Office, 1988.

Johnston, W. B. *Workforce 2000: Work and Workers for the 21st Century.* Indianapolis, Ind.: Hudson Institute, 1987. 143 pp. (ED 290 887)

Magruder, D. R. "Community College and Business Partnerships: A Statewide Model Skills Program." *Journal of Studies in Technical Careers,* 1988, 10 (3), 239–249.

24   ECONOMIC AND WORK FORCE DEVELOPMENT

National Governors' Association. *Time for Results: The Governors' Report on Education.*
Washington, D.C.: National Governors' Association, 1986. 53 pp. (ED 279 610)
National Governors' Association. *Jobs, Growth, and Competitiveness: Productive People,
Productive Policies.* Washington, D.C.: National Governors' Association, 1987.
107 pp. (ED 290 350)
Newman, F. *Choosing Quality: Reducing Conflict Between the State and the University.*
Denver, Colo.: Education Commission of the States, 1987. 135 pp. (ED 305 848)
Parnell, D. *The Neglected Majority.* Washington, D.C.: American Association of Com-
munity and Junior Colleges, 1985.
Tillery, D., and Wattenbarger, J. L. "State Power in a New Era: Threats to Local
Authority." In W. L. Deegan and J. F. Gollattscheck (eds.), *Ensuring Effective Gov-
ernance.* New Directions for Community Colleges, no. 49. San Francisco: Jossey-
Bass, 1985.
Tschechtelin, J. D. "High Tech and the Community College." *SBCC Bulletin,* 1988,
18 (1), 1.
Waddell, G. "Tips for Training a World-Class Work Force." *Community, Technical,
and Junior College Journal,* 1990, *60* (4), 21–27.
W. T. Grant Foundation. *The Forgotten Half: Pathways to Success for America's Youth
and Young Families.* Washington, D.C.: William T. Grant Foundation Commission
on Work, Family, and Citizenship, 1988. 201 pp. (ED 300 580)

*Lawrence A. Nespoli is executive director of the New Jersey Council of County
Colleges in Trenton, New Jersey.*

The practice of hosting quasi-independent entities, such as Small Business Development Centers, which focus on economic and work force development, requires clarification of small business administration and college goals.

Meeting Small Business Needs Through Small Business Development Centers

Janice B. Carmichael

Extensive growth and expansion of America's small businesses have dominated economic statistics for the past several years. New American jobs have largely been an outcome of small business. For example, there were 522,247 new incorporations between January and September 1988 (U.S. Small Business Administration, 1988). Slower growth, however, is expected for small businesses in the 1990s since consumers are expected to spend less, in turn directly affecting small businesses such as construction companies and retail and wholesale dealers. More effort will be spent on management training and creative marketing.

Declining numbers in the labor force makes retention and competition for employees one of the major issues of the 1990s. The demand for greater efficiency and productivity to meet labor shortages goes hand in hand with the expansion of new technologies and computer usage. Small business owners need to know how to schedule and stock inventories to offset the fluctuating demand for products.

Having found that entry-level workers lack basic math and reading skills, employers have been forced to invest in training in order to attract and retain staff. In seeking cost-effective methods for training employees, many small businesses are turning to the local community college. While not all of their problems can be solved in the classroom, many can be anticipated and possibly prevented.

Small Business Development Centers

Small Business Development Centers (SBDCs) were created by an act of Congress under P.L. 86-302 in 1980 and amended by P.L. 98-395 in 1984. They

NEW DIRECTIONS FOR COMMUNITY COLLEGES, no. 75, Fall 1991 © Jossey-Bass Inc., Publishers

are a venture funded jointly by the federal government, through the U.S. Small Business Administration (SBA), and public and private agencies at state and local levels. Designed to help those interested in starting a business and providing management assistance for those already in business, SBDCs offer counseling, education and training programs, and information and referral services by professional consultants. SBDCs have directly contributed to the support and expansion of economic development programs. They have shown that a public-private partnership linking education, business, and government is not only possible but highly beneficial to all parties.

Community Colleges and SBDCs

Community colleges were invited early to participate in the SBDC program since their commitment to the community and their grass-roots approach to education made them a natural choice. Originally, 6 community colleges were chosen as "lead centers." Today, 114 community colleges host SBDCs.

While community colleges may not be able to provide the research-oriented partnerships that universities can offer, most have been offering important training services to local business and industry since the early 1980s (Powers, Powers, Betz, and Aslanian, 1988). While the majority of these programs emphasize educational services to the work force, they have established an important track record for colleges wishing to establish SBDCs. They typically cater to adult students who are returning to college to update skills, reenter the work force, receive professional instruction, or explore new career options.

These programs are offered generally by continuing education, community services, technical training, and vocational education and cooperative education divisions. Most are tailored to local or regional needs. Several departments at community colleges have already established small business assistance centers in conjunction with their business and industry outreach programs.

Establishing an SBDC in a Community College

One should not assume that an SBDC will automatically fit into the overall mission of a community college. While community colleges are known for their responsiveness to local education needs, the hosting of a quasi-independent entity focused on economic development requires clarification of both SBA and college goals.

First Step: Gaining Internal Commitments. It is recommended that the college establish a task force to investigate the feasibility of hosting an SBDC. One of the most important questions that this task force must ask is whether there is a consensus and commitment to economic development among the leaders of the college.

An important job of the task force is to prepare a preliminary profile and *needs assessment* of the local small business community. Data on the labor force, the types of businesses, and economic indicators are usually available through local and state offices of economic development, park and planning commissions, and chambers of commerce. Identification and analysis of existing community programs serving small business can alleviate any potential conflict between the college and community programs as well as identify potential support.

When the college has made a commitment to addressing the issues of economic development, the decision to develop an SBDC must take into account the compatibility with existing programs and department politics. University-based SBDCs are most often affiliated with business schools. Community college programs are more often partnered with divisions of continuing education or community services. This partnership requires considerable planning and a clear delineation of responsibilities in order to ensure that the respective programs work together in an effective way.

Internal commitments must be balanced by *external commitments*. There are many people in the private sector who do not understand or appreciate higher education's commitment to economic development. In order to enhance the visibility and credibility of the SBDC, college officials and SBDC directors must agree to become involved in local and state economic development efforts.

Colleges should be alert to potential political problems in establishing ties with the business community. SBDCs depend greatly on private-sector volunteers, many of whom have their own professional and personal agendas. Perceived competition with the private sector is the most often cited obstacle to a productive partnership.

The college will need to determine whether it is prepared to make a *financial commitment*. SBDCs must match federal funds: one-half in kind and one-half in cash. If colleges intend to use local, state, and private-sector cash or in-kind donations, these must be assessed and factored into the match in funds.

The joint tasks of meeting match requirements and providing quarterly and annual budget reports require extensive time and personnel. While SBDC directors may have the responsibility of allocating individual line items, the monitoring of funds is usually relegated to the college finance office. Program managers and financial officers must keep accurate records of expenses and program-generated income in order to meet grant obligations.

In summary, internal capabilities and cooperation must be carefully compared with external cooperation and community need. At this point the task force will either be disbanded or take on a new role, that of the planning committee.

Second Step: Developing a Plan of Action. When it has been determined that the college is willing to commit the necessary time and resources to the development of an SBDC, the next step is to determine a plan of action with a timetable and identify key players for implementation. Many colleges create a smaller and more manageable planning committee at this time. Many SBDCs have indicated that the planning advisory committees were essential to their success.

Many small business development officers stress the critical importance of having the business community involved directly in the planning process. Several colleges have held small business forums, inviting members of local chambers of commerce, Rotary and Lions clubs, service organizations, and others. In addition, colleges can tap many of the existing SBA programs such as the Service Corps of Retired Executives and the Active Corps of Executives. By making these groups a part of the foundation of the SBDC program, support can be gained.

SBDCs across the country are providing solutions to small business problems and responding to the needs of small business in many positive ways. The case studies that follow highlight three major community-college-based SBDCs. These centers were selected because of their exemplary delivery of services. Each SBDC was sent a fifteen-question survey and a letter arranging for a follow-up interview with the center director. Without exception, the SBDCs share one strong common bond: an almost missionary zeal and dedication to working with small businesses.

Lane Community College, Eugene, Oregon

Oregon has the first community-college-based network in the nation. Modeled after Lane Community College's Business Assistance Center, the network is funded by state, federal, host institution, and private-sector funds. Additional supplemental grants, state lottery funds, and a Sears Partnership Development grant make it one of the most cost-effective and productive SBDC networks in the country. Also, Lane is considered one of the most innovative and creative SBDCs in the country.

Located in a remodeled department store, Lane's downtown center enjoys strong support from its administration and the twenty-thousand-strong businesses and industries in the community. The center has office space, counseling rooms, classrooms, a library resource center, and a forty-five-client conference facility fully enhanced with a satellite down-link and multiple viewing locations. International educational programs provide experiences for Costa Rican, Jamaican, and Guatemalan business representatives through cooperation with the U.S. Aid to International Development Program.

Mercer County Community College, Trenton, New Jersey

One of the first pilot SBDC programs funded by the SBA is the New Jersey Small Business Development Network. The New Jersey Department of Commerce and Economic Development, Division of Small Business, Women and Minority Businesses provides funding in addition to the federal SBA funds. The Port Authority of New York/New Jersey supports the funding of an Air Services Development Office to facilitate contracts between local businesses and the airport.

The Mercer Community College SBDC is typical of programs affiliated with continuing education divisions. It has achieved national as well as regional fame. Known as the primary resource in Mercer County for business information, the SBDC emphasizes practical academic assistance, cooperative ventures, quality service that goes the extra mile, and visibility through public awareness and participation. It makes a special effort to communicate with its constituency through a monthly newsletter, *Small Business Review*. Community volunteerism at the SBDC is strong. Over one hundred community small business consultants and four senior counselors provide volunteer services.

Mercer's director stresses that its success as an SBDC is tied to the good chemistry between it and the college, the local chambers of commerce, the lead center at Rutgers, and the Mercer Office of Economic Development. Flexibility and visibility are key ingredients. Quality programs and satisfied clients make Mercer one of the more notable programs.

Montgomery Community College, Montgomery County, Maryland

One of six SBDCs serving the Washington, D.C., metropolitan region, and part of the Howard University network, this center receives funding from the Washington office of SBA, with matching funds provided by the college's Office of Continuing Education. It will enter the new State of Maryland SBDC network in October 1991 as part of a tricounty consortium arrangement.

Addressing the complex needs of a large and dispersed cosmopolitan business community, near the nation's capital, with one of the highest per capita incomes in the country and a 2 percent unemployment rate, this SBDC faces constant challenges. The SBDC has a fully-equipped computer room available for training. A high-technology computer bulletin board, Ed-Link, is maintained by the SBDC in a joint venture with the Montgomery County High-Technology Council. The network also maintains a computer program to track SBDC clients and monitor training programs.

Like Lane and Mercer's SBDCs, Montgomery College was chosen by the Internal Revenue Service to offer a year-long pilot program of tax assistance. The prebusiness certificate programs emphasize planning and management skills for start-up businesses and entrepreneurs. A nine-month Small Business Enterprise Program caters to more established business.

A cable TV series, "Small Business: Myth or Reality," focused each of twelve half-hour talk shows on topical issues of concern to local small businesses. Typically, a counselor and an SBDC client joined the director in the discussions.

Co-sponsored events include a Home-Based Business Day, with the National Association of Home-Based Businesses, and a popular International Trade series, offered with the Maryland Office of International Trade. A joint conference with the Montgomery County public schools on Kids in Business teaches young entrepreneurs about small business. The 1989 Women Business Advocate of the Year Award was sponsored by the SBDC. Montgomery College's SBDC director arranged for the initial matches between mentors and protégées in the Washington, D.C., area Women's Network for Entrepreneurial Training Program, a national effort to strengthen women-owned businesses. Recent efforts in the Hispanic community have resulted in programs and counseling in Spanish and a joint venture with the First American Bank.

Conclusion

SBDCs offer means for meeting small business development needs, and thus economic development needs. Communities with SBDCs report that the programs have a positive impact on the economic growth of regional small business. Further, SBDCs are an added attraction for businesses wishing to locate in a region. Also, the presence of an SBDC can help stimulate private-sector investment and assistance where it may not have existed before.

SBDCs across the country are providing solutions to small business problems. Partnerships have been built that will even outlast the SBDCs.

References

Powers, D. R., Powers, M. F., Betz, F., and Aslanian, C. B. *Higher Education in Partnership with Industry: Opportunities and Strategies for Training, Research, and Economic Development.* San Francisco: Jossey-Bass, 1988.

U.S. Small Business Administration, Office of Advocacy. *The State of Small Business, A Report to the President.* Washington, D.C.: Government Printing Office, 1988.

Janice B. Carmichael is director of the Montgomery Community College Center for Small Business in Montgomery County, Maryland.

How can we assist those communities with low levels of new-business formation? How do we turn around declining rural economies?

Developing Rural Business Incubators

Mark L. Weinberg, DeLysa Burnier

Expansion of the role of community colleges in economic development has been adopted as a formal goal by the American Association of Community and Junior Colleges (American Association of Community and Junior Colleges, 1989). One focus of these development activities is the encouragement of small business. Small Business Development Centers are operated by approximately 40 percent of community colleges in small communities and rural areas (see Carmichael, this volume, for some examples of Small Business Development Centers). A small number are involved in *business incubators* either on or off campus (Donato, 1988).

A business incubator is a facility where shared services and business and management assistance are provided for tenant companies. These services and assistance are usually in exchange for rent (often at below-market rates), fees for services, a percentage of sales or royalties, or equity in the company. Incubators are owned and operated by public and private organizations. Although similar types of organizations operate incubators in rural and urban areas, the distribution of management of the facilities varies significantly between rural and urban areas.

Academic institutions, universities, and community and technical colleges own and manage the majority of these facilities in rural areas. While

The authors appreciate the assistance of Margaret Thomas, Midwest Research Institute; David N. Allen, Pennsylvania State University; Anthony Zeiss, president, Pueblo Community College; Susan Reynaud, American Association of Community and Junior Colleges; James Breagy, National Council for Urban Economic Development; and incubator officials who provided information about their programs. The views expressed are those of the authors only.

the total number of rural incubators owned or managed by community and technical colleges is small, these colleges play a significant role in incubator development in rural areas.

Community colleges have formed incubators on campus by remodeling unused facilities or building new ones, or by leasing buildings off campus (Donato, 1988; Waddell, 1990). Community colleges can assist in the establishment of private nonprofit corporations and community-based incubators and provide counseling or technical assistance to the community-based incubators (Donato, 1988).

This chapter discusses community college incubation efforts in rural America. First, rural incubation as an entrepreneurial and small business development strategy is discussed. Next, community college participation in the incubation process is examined, and examples of community college incubation efforts are provided. Finally, recommendations for community college participation are offered.

Rural Entrepreneurship and Incubation in the United States

Many economic development practitioners view entrepreneurship as a key to successful economic development. Birch (1987, p. 16) has shown that firms with fewer than twenty employees created about 88 percent of all net new jobs in the U.S. economy from 1981 to 1985.

Does rural America share in this entrepreneurial growth? According to Birch, "remote" areas, that is, rural areas at least sixty miles away from the nearest metropolitan area, witnessed the growth of 281,000 new businesses between 1978 and 1987. New business start-ups in these areas tend to focus on basic needs (that is, food service), revolve around national resources (that is, environmental businesses), provide goods or services needed because of the area's remoteness (that is, health care services), or offer practical benefits no matter how remotely located (that is, packaging plants) (Birch, 1987, pp. 14–15).

Additionally, several studies of enterprise development in states such as Minnesota, Iowa, North Dakota (Popovich and Buss, 1989), and Maine show that this national rate of job creation also holds for nonmetropolitan areas (Popovich, 1988). "Between 1980 and 1986, 19,797 new enterprises created 108,057 new jobs in Iowa"; rural areas of Iowa shared "fully in employment growth associated with the successful formation of new businesses. Rural and agricultural counties in Iowa kept pace with other areas" (Popovich and Buss, 1987, p. 3).

However, many nonmetropolitan areas are not as competitive as metropolitan areas in terms of the factors that generate enterprise creation. Although rural areas do well in factors that influence manufacturing plant location, "they are notably short on capital, entrepreneurial climate, suitable management advice, and business services for new firms" (Malecki, 1988, p. 21).

How then do we promote and protect entrepreneurship or assist those communities with low levels of new business formation? How do we turn around declining rural economies? Experts on rural entrepreneurship recommend that rural communities (1) develop entrepreneur identification programs and gear business management skills programs to these individuals, (2) develop strategies that focus on identifying gaps in local markets that new small businesses could fill, (3) provide expanded financing for risk-oriented ventures, (4) develop information networks for entrepreneurs, (5) reduce regulation and paperwork requirements for small businesses, and (6) structure technical assistance programs to serve entrepreneurial clients (Popovich and Buss, 1987).

The development of business incubators fits well within these guidelines for the types of entrepreneurial programs that rural communities should pursue (Weinberg, 1987). Some have argued that incubators may replace the industrial park as a rural development strategy (for example, Plosila, 1988). However, incubators are not a panacea for economic development. They should be considered only as one option in a comprehensive, entrepreneurial and business development strategy for local communities.

Rural Incubators

Incubators differ from other entrepreneurial development strategies in that they offer comprehensive business assistance services and business network capabilities to start-up and young firms in an interactive environment within a single facility (Campbell, 1988). Incubators work with entrepreneurs to accelerate the development of emerging companies and reduce the risk of business failure by assisting small businesses in the early stages of growth.

They add value to their tenants' businesses by providing inexpensive office space and proximity to other entrepreneurs in a creative entrepreneurial environment. Incubators also provide shared office services, business and technology assistance, access to financing, and a network of connections inside and outside the incubator (Allen and Bazan, 1989b).

While the economic development potential of incubators is high, the record of incubator development both nationally and in rural areas is mixed. Employment in tenant firms is generally low. Incubator periods for tenant companies are generally short, with the average tenancy in facilities at two years. Firm success rates are generally high with an average of two tenant graduates to every one who discontinues operation. Local retention of graduate firms is generally high, about 85 percent (Allen, 1989).

The record of incubator development and effectiveness varies among facilities. In general, incubators are high-risk development ventures for several reasons. First, there was an early rush to promote and develop incubators as viable entrepreneurial development projects. As such, many projects were ill-conceived and poorly planned, an unfortunate circumstance that still undermines many of these ventures. Second, management of an incubator facility requires a unique set of skills, and incubator managers are in short supply. Manager training has been offered only recently, and educational and associational support mechanisms are still developing. Third, lack of success in effectiveness, as measured by the extent to which incubators add value to tenant companies, also comes from a complex series of planning and management issues. For example, few incubator programs successfully link development and operation activities or concentrate on the real estate aspect of incubators, both central to business development activities.

These problems plague incubators whether they are located in urban or rural areas. Of special significance to rural areas are the issues of marketing and finance. The task of marketing the incubator facility is different for rural areas because of the number and types of start-up firms. Rural areas often lack an adequate client base of single-facility incubator firms. To achieve a critical mass of firms for incubator operation, several communities may have to jointly develop a facility.

Community Colleges and Rural Incubation

Currently, there are several models of incubation in rural areas: traditional single facilities, regional incubators, and incubation systems. Community college participation spans the range of these incubation activities, as shown in Exhibit 4.1. In 1987 only two community or junior colleges were identified by the National Business Incubation Association (NBIA) as having incubators. By the end of 1989, fourteen community or junior colleges and systems had incubators or incubator-type facilities (Waddell, 1990; Montgomery, Morgan, Myers, 1989; NBIA, 1989). The number of incubators in the United States was 360 at the end of 1989, up from 45 in 1983.

Community college incubators are located in large cities and small rural communities. Most college incubators are run by the college or operated as private nonprofit facilities. Additionally, some community colleges operate regional incubators or incubator systems.

Incubator systems include the North Arkansas Community College System in Salem, Arkansas, and Des Moines Area Community College–Circle West in Audubon, Iowa. The following cases illustrate the different models of incubation at community colleges.

Community College Incubator: Labette Community College (Parsons, Kansas). (Personal communication Margaret Thomas, April 14, 1989, and Mark Turnball, April 14, 1989.) This business industrial center is located south of Kansas City in Parsons, Kansas. Labette Community

Exhibit 4.1. Community College Incubators and Incubation Systems

College and Location
North Arkansas Community College, Salem, Arkansas[a]
John Woods Community College, Quincy, Illinois
Rose-Hulman Institute of Technology, Terre Haute, Indiana
Kirkwood Community College, Marion, Iowa
Labette Community College, Parsons, Kansas
Roanoke-Chowan Technical College, Ahoskie, North Carolina
Kiamichi Area Vocational Technical Schools System, Durant, Atoka, Hugo,
    McAlester, Poteau, Stigler, and Idabel, Oklahoma
Oklahoma State University, Technical Branch, Okmulgee, Oklahoma
Houston Community College, Stafford, Texas
University of Houston, Victoria, Texas
Dallas County College District, Dallas, Texas
University of Wisconsin, Stout, Wisconsin
Milwaukee Area Technical College, Milwaukee, Wisconsin
Southside Virginia Community College, Keysville, Virginia
Des Moines Area Community College–Golden Circle, Des Moines, Iowa
Des Moines Area Community College–Circle West, Audubon, Iowa.

[a] The North Arkansas Business Incubator System is only loosely affiliated with the North Arkansas Community College. The college is located ninety miles from the facility. The incubator is affiliated with the college because incubator funding in Arkansas comes from the Arkansas Science and Technology Authority. Funds under this program are restricted to institutions of higher learning. The center provides incubator services to small manufacturing companies and start-ups in a fifteen-county area of north-central Arkansas. It is organized as a private nonprofit corporation. The center anticipates that the college will provide accounting assistance to clients and work toward the development of an entrepreneurial outreach program.
Source: Montgomery, Morgan, and Myers, 1989, pp. 13–14.

College serves the southeast corner of Kansas, which has an overall population of forty-eight thousand. The area's economy is agricultural, with manufacturing in wood and metal fabrication. The railroad merger with Union Pacific resulted in a loss of 400 jobs, however, and the closing of a munitions factory resulted in 560 layoffs.

The college is a publicly supported institution with a full-time student-equivalent enrollment of about thirteen hundred. In addition to the economic benefits of the facility, the college operates the incubator as a source of employment for its students, as a source for the training services of the college, and as a means to promote the college's community image.

Initially, operating funds came from the college and a three-year grant from the Kansas Department of Education. Funds for facility renovation came from an Economic Development Authority grant, the Labette County Economic Development Commission, and public match and private match grants.

The incubator provides shared business services to clients. Unlike many incubators, the facility also provides production assistance, including production planning, inventory control, and quality control. The center currently has four tenants. Two businesses failed because they joined the incubator at too early a stage of development, before sufficient assistance was available.

The incubator is linked to Jobs Inc., a private nonprofit corporation that provides local seed capital to start up companies. The college also started an entrepreneurial development program.

Regional Incubators: Rural Enterprise Inc. and Kiamichi Area Vocational Technical Schools System. An illustration of a regional system with incubator facilities is the alliance between Rural Enterprises Inc. (REI) and the Kiamichi Area Vocational Technical Schools System (KAVTS). REI is headquartered in Durant, Oklahoma, and the KAVTS facilities are located throughout the state.

REI was established as a nonprofit corporation in 1980 to promote entrepreneurial development in southeastern Oklahoma. Facilities at the vocational technical schools range in size from 4,800 square feet to 7,200 square feet. Currently, each facility is set up for only one tenant.

Tenants receive support services from REI, Oklahoma State Department of Vocational Technical Education, Kiamichi Area Vocational Technical Schools System, and the federal Job Training Partnership Act. Services include graduate rent, financial packaging, and technical assistance. REI screens applicants for the facilities and provides follow-up technical assistance.

The facilities are part of the vocational technical schools, and they use the incubators to create jobs for their students as well as to promote the economic welfare of the community. The program is being expanded to other areas of the state through Oklahoma's vocational technical schools system.

Regional Incubation System: Circle West, Des Moines Area Community College. An example of a rural incubation system is Circle West, operated by the Des Moines Area Community College (DMACC) (Joe Robbins, personal communication, April 14, 1989). The college also operates a single facility, Golden Circle, and serves an eleven-county area in central Iowa, encompassing 117 communities. The area chose an incubation system strategy because individual communities in the area are too small to support their own incubators. The area served by the Circle West facility is a seven-county area within a fifty-mile radius. Circle West acts as an administrative center and is located in leased space of a United Telephone Company facility. The incubator provides information on vacant space in the seven-county area and works with businesses to match space to needs. Satellite offices will be located in six counties and in the city of Audubon.

Services are provided under a program similar to the passport system development offered by Southwestern Pennsylvania Economic Development District. Companies are given passports that provide access to clerical and consulting services on a fee basis. Clients are given passports that enable them to receive service from providers in the area. These providers include economic development groups, private businesses, and chambers of commerce. The program director's position is funded from a three-year state grant, DMACC funds, and a local match grant. Marketing is handled through entrepreneurial outreach programs and through informal referrals by community organizations affiliated with Circle West.

Recommendations and Conclusions

Community colleges usually start incubators to promote economic development (business and job creation) in a community. In addition to a college's contribution to the economic welfare of the community or region, a community college incubator can contribute to the education and training missions of the college. This contribution is often achieved by linking the incubator program to cooperative education, internships, student placement, customized training, and entrepreneurial outreach programs.

However, the missions of business incubator programs (with their focus on entrepreneurial development) and of education and training are also significantly different. The educational mission is based on the idea of equal educational opportunity, which is achieved by providing students with education and skills training. Entrepreneurs, in contrast to the traditional client base for community colleges, have different needs and objectives. For example, the provision of customized training for industry is very different from the highly specialized training needs of small businesses. Additionally, the services and capabilities of community colleges that are related to their educational programming may not be best suited to or most needed by tenant companies in incubators. Community colleges may not be experienced in linking entrepreneurial start-ups to the financial and business development community. Development of these linkages is accomplished through creation of an advisory board for the incubator.

An alternative to community college ownership and operation of the facility is the creation of a private nonprofit corporation. Most community college incubators are organized as private nonprofit corporations. In these arrangements the college is the principal or one major partner in the corporation. According to James Montgomery at the Milwaukee Area Technical College (Montgomery, Morgan, and Myers, 1989), a private nonprofit arrangement provides a flexible mechanism for business development or venture and it allows for greater participation by important community groups than in for-profit arrangements.

Minimization of risk in incubator development is difficult since incubators are by definition risk-taking organizations. Community colleges do increase their risk in incubator ventures when they lack experience in two key elements of incubator development: real estate management and the provision of assistance to entrepreneurial start-ups. When the community college lacks experience in these areas, it may be more appropriate to pursue alternative entrepreneurial development programs that provide business development services to community entrepreneurs, or to develop an entrepreneurial outreach program or an incubation system. The incubator may be a natural outgrowth of these programs, and the college would have a greater reservoir of experience for running these types of business development programs.

Development of incubator programs should include a discussion of the relationship between the community economic development goals and the educational goals of the college. Officials should examine the appropriate structure and market niche for the incubator, the relationship between the development and operations process of the facility, and the role that the college and development partners play. A realistic understanding of the management, limits, and development problems of incubator programs and the linkage of the incubator to other development programs in the community is warranted also.

References

Allen, D. N. "The State of the Business Incubator Industry." Unpublished manuscript, Department of Higher Education, Pennsylvania State University, 1989.

Allen, D. N., and Bazan, E. J. "Evaluation of Multi-Tenant Buildings as a Component in Local Economic Recovery. Parts 1-2: Policy Analysis." Report prepared for the U.S. Department of Commerce, Economic Development Administration, Athens, Ohio, 1989.

American Association of Community and Junior Colleges. "1989 Public Policy Agenda." *Community, Technical, and Junior College Journal*, 1989, *59* (3), 19-26.

Birch, D. *Job Creation in America*. New York: Free Press, 1987.

Campbell, C. *Change Agents in the New Economy: Business Incubators and Economic Development*. Minneapolis, Minn.: Cooperative Community Development Program, Hubert H. Humphrey Institute of Public Affairs, 1988.

Donato, D. J. "Economic Development." In *Small/Rural Community Colleges*. Report of the Commission on Small/Rural Community Colleges. Washington, D.C.: American Association of Community and Junior Colleges, 1988.

Malecki, E. J. "New Firm Start-Ups: Key to Rural Growth." *Rural Development Perspectives*, 1988, *4* (2), 18-23.

Montgomery, J., Morgan, J., and Myers, J. *An Introduction to Developing an Urban Business Incubator*. Washington, D.C.: American Association of Community and Junior Colleges, 1989. 40 pp. (ED 312 001)

National Business Incubation Association (NBIA). *NBIA Directory of NBIA Members*. Athens, Ohio: NBIA, 1989.

Plosila, W. H. "Technical Innovation and Economic Development." *Entrepreneurial Economy*, 1988, *6* (5), 9-11.

Popovich, M. *New Businesses, Entrepreneurship, and Rural Development: Building a State Strategy*. Washington, D.C.: Council of State Policy and Planning Agencies, 1988.

Popovich, M. G., and Buss, T. F. *Rural Enterprise Development: An Iowa Case Study*. Washington, D.C.: Council of State Policy and Planning Agencies, 1987.

Popovich, M. G., and Buss, T. F. "Entrepreneurs Find Niche Even in Rural America." *Rural Development Perspectives*, 1989, *5* (3), 11-14.

Thomas, M. *A Portfolio of Community College Initiatives in Rural Economic Development.* Kansas City, Kan.: Midwest Research Institute, 1989.

Waddell, G. "Tips for Training a World-Class Work Force." *Community, Technical, and Junior College Journal,* 1990, *60* (4), 21–27.

Mark L. Weinberg is a professor in the Department of Political Science at Ohio University, Athens.

DeLysa Burnier is an assistant professor in the Department of Political Science at Ohio University, Athens.

Community college presidents who wish to become leaders in economic development need to know their environments and to recognize clearly what types of growth are appropriate to and should be fostered in their communities.

Assuming a Leadership Role in Community Economic Development

Robert J. Kopecek

Conditions that foster and stimulate economic growth occur only with strong and dynamic leadership and with a broad-based community partnership. This chapter focuses on the leadership role that college presidents can play in regional, nonprofit economic development organizations.

Community college presidents must support activities aimed at fostering environments that encourage developers to invest new money in their communities and to help existing firms grow. Similarly, these presidents must give leadership to community-based, nonprofit economic development organizations that make available low-priced developed land, capital, skilled labor, and ample and low-cost power and transportation. In addition, leaders who wish to see economic development occur must be concerned with the expansion of infrastructure, creation or expansion of water and sewer systems, disposition of solid waste, development of roads and highways, competitive tax structures, establishment of equitable zoning regulations, development of industrial parks, provision of competitive financing packages, and active, ongoing regional marketing programs that clearly demonstrate why the targeted communities are good places to live, work, and raise a family.

Types of Economic Development

Two types of economic development are likely to occur in a region. The more glamorous of the two is concerned with attracting new industries to an area or stimulating expansion of existing businesses. With this type of development comes the creation of many new jobs, construction of new buildings, new industrial parks, new roads, and new parks and schools. This type of development is dynamic and exciting.

Economic development of the second type is more typical. New businesses are attracted periodically to a region, and the emphasis is on maintaining companies and producing a climate where the efficiency, effectiveness, and competitiveness of existing firms are enhanced. The goal in this scenario is to foster a climate where companies will add new product lines periodically, gradually increase production and sales, add a few new people annually, and occasionally build extensions to their existing buildings.

Assertions

Economic development is as much a political process within a community as it is a series of business decisions. Development depends as much on the political attitudes, aspirations, and vision of elected local and state officials as it does on businessmen and businesswomen. The history of regions that have experienced long-term economic growth since World War II demonstrates that economic development flourishes and is sustained in areas where there is a partnership between business, government, and education. Leaders of these segments need to be committed to the task of fostering development in order for it to occur.

What specifically needs to be done in a community to cause growth greatly depends on local conditions. In the northeast, especially in the Northampton area of Pennsylvania, for example, the presence of many small and provincial municipal governments (towns, boroughs, and villages), along with an equal number of zoning boards, sewer and water authorities, and police, fire, and emergency squads, makes the climate difficult for developers and existing businesses. Initiation and maintenance of a countywide planning and marketing effort require a high degree of coordination, an effective broad-based organization, a small but professional staff, money, and the commitment of the community's business and governmental leaders.

It is also very helpful to have state government equally dedicated to the task of fostering growth. National and multinational corporations assess business climate in the aggregate. Businesses look to the performance of relatively large geographical regions by studying statewide indicators. When attempting to attract large firms, local leaders are well served when the state has an aggressive marketing plan supported by a governor with the will and discretionary power to help make a transaction happen.

Business leaders want access to education, and in most areas where major expansion is occurring, the educational tie, especially to research universities, is evident. Many other business factors, however, such as the availability of land, water, sewers, affordable labor, low taxes, good transportation, and the favorability of the state's policies toward unions and employee benefits, are usually perceived by business executives as more important than training and even university-based research.

According to Katsinas and Lacey (1989, pp. 13–14), there appear to be five major reasons that business executives are increasingly looking to community colleges for creative local responses to changing economic needs: (1) recognition of the community college as a source of assimilation assistance to new immigrants to a region, (2) recognition of the need for new directions to expand and diversify a given local economy in response to the economic disruptions of the early 1980s, (3) recognition of flaws in federal and state employment assistance and job-training policies in the larger context of economic and demographic change, (4) recognition of shortcomings in current American political ideology that can prevent community colleges from rising to their full capacity in economically assisting their service areas, and (5) recognition that community colleges (as community-based institutions) constitute a delivery system already in place to provide new programs and services. Katsinas and Lacey suggest that of these five reasons for turning to community colleges for leadership, the last is the most important.

Assumptions

Presidents who wish to become leaders in economic development need to know their environments and to recognize clearly what kind of growth they seek to foster and nurture. Each president should be satisfied that the stimulation of economic development is consistent with the philosophy, mission, and goals of his or her college, and that the college community, and the community at large, will accept the president's commitment to efforts that are not directly related to the day-to-day operations of the college.

Situations in which these supportive attitudes may not exist are easily identified. The following situations are illustrative: (1) The people of a rural county, whose economic base is agricultural or recreational, may well perceive economic development, or at least the attraction of new manufacturing firms, as fundamentally undesirable. People in this setting might argue that good land would be diverted, many people would have to be imported, and the current quality of life would be changed negatively. In an environment of this type, a community college president—if he or she thinks that change should occur—should strive to become a well-informed resource person. To do more might be counterproductive. According to MacDougall and Friedlander (1989, p. 259), "If the leader is too far in front of his or her constituents, a lack of support can result in negative effects (costs) for the college's leadership." (2) In suburban areas where the increased needs for infrastructure, schools, and other services have been created by previous economic development activities, citizens may perceive additional growth as threatening. They may see additional economic development only in terms of increased traffic, congestion, crime, taxes, and big-city problems. A president's involvement in this community's economic development is thus rendered difficult. Conditions like this exist in some communities in New Jersey, Pennsylvania, and the New England states. (3) Additionally, people in a county may recognize the need for economic development, but the college community and the community at large may not perceive the college or its president as an appropriate active player. The specific climate and traditions of the institution may run counter to the active involvement of any of its members in any community activity that is not directly connected to a narrow definition of education or to the day-to-day operation of the college. It could happen, albeit to the detriment of the total community, that in this situation the college president cannot become involved.

All three of these examples clearly illustrate the basic point that the community college president, even when motivated by the best of intentions, is well advised to know the community! If conditions are not favorable, the president might consider other ways to provide leadership. As one college president has indicated, "You want to be pushed by the followers, and not be so far out in front that you can't pull them with you. It does not matter what kind of a visionary mission the leader has; if the leader is not closely in touch with the followers, the leader will have a problem" (MacDougall and Friedlander, 1989, p. 259).

Getting Started

How does one get involved? Given the variety of organizations, agencies, and structures promoting economic development in communities across the nation, there obviously is no single point of entry. Further, it is unlikely that the involvement will initially be all-consuming. The voluntary aspects of nonprofit economic development activities are similar to those of other community organization activities. Involvement begins slowly. The ascribed status of the president's position, however, should be sufficient to allow appointment or election to an appropriate board or committee. The task of establishing a broad-based, communitywide group, if none exists, would be of great value to the community and more difficult to accomplish.

Many business representatives still do not believe that "an academic person" is willing to work on business or governmental problems not directly related to education. As with all groups, these initial concerns dissipate quickly when the individual does a competent job. As one college president discovered, "You have to deliver on what you say and promise. Otherwise, you lose your credibility. Once you lose your credibility, staff are reluctant to put out energy to follow in other categories" (MacDougall and Friedlander, 1989, p. 259).

Necessity of an Organization

A broad-based organization that brings together the leadership of the community is an absolute necessity. It must enjoy the endorsement and involvement of key political and business leaders, including representatives of major banks. The specific function or objective of the organization should be to plan and market and to provide a one-stop information service. Its more important task, however, is to be the integrating force that gives continuity to efforts to provide a favorable climate in which economic growth and expansion can occur. When an organization of this type exists, the community college president should join it. If it does not exist, then he or she should work to establish it.

Elements of Growth and Development

The community college president, working within a broad-based community organization with other community leaders, should foster the following essential elements of development: (1) Many developers argue that there are three keys to economic development: location, location, and location. Although it may be easier in some places than in others, virtually every community can be creatively marketed for some specific type of business or industry. Community leaders must carefully and honestly assess the advantages offered by their particular geographical locale and find ways to appeal to specific industries. (2) It is essential that developers and existing businesses have the opportunity to secure competitive, conventional bank loans and the full array of tax-free instruments. (3) A community must have available labor and the means to provide in-service training on a continuing basis. (4) Competitively priced, developed land must be available. (5) State economic development initiatives must be available. And (6) there should be a mechanism for addressing regional (multicounty) business and economic issues.

Most business, infrastructure, and labor questions do not stop at county boundaries; thus, a mechanism for a regional business climate needs to be established and maintained. For example, the Lehigh Valley Partnership in Pennsylvania is an informal organization that identifies critical questions and focuses attention on alternative solutions in the Lehigh Valley region. Also located in Pennsylvania, the Ben Franklin Partnership has become the largest annual technological innovation program in the nation and has generated more private-sector matching funds than has any similar program in the country. Success of this program can be measured by the fact that 244 new firms were started and 175 were expanded during the first thirty-four months of the partnership (Plosila, 1987).

Conclusion

The activities involved in fostering economic growth and development in an area are all interrelated and intertwined. Planned programs and community action, aimed at creating a climate that encourages the growth and maintenance of economic well-being, are necessary, and community college presidents can provide leadership. Most presidents, because of their interests, training, and experience, are naturals for this leadership role.

Although conditions vary, local leaders interested in nurturing growth and development need to address all issues that affect the climate for growth. Developers and the executives of existing firms need to know that the community is responsive to their needs. Communities need to marshall, foster, and improve those elements that encourage job creation and retention. The patterns of organizational development that emerge will be different across local regions, but an integrated, planned, and coordinated developmental effort is the common goal. Since the well-being of community colleges is directly related to local economic well-being, the active involvement of the community college president, in most communities, is highly desirable.

References

Katsinas, S. G., and Lacey, V. A. *Community Colleges and Economic Development: Models of Institutional Effectiveness.* Washington, D.C.: American Association of Community and Junior Colleges, 1989. 97 pp. (ED 312 006)

MacDougall, P. R., and Friedlander, J. H. "The Costs of Innovation." In T. O'Banion (ed.), *Innovation in the Community College.* New York: American Council on Education/Macmillan, 1989. 294 pp. (ED 305 981)

Plosila, W. H. *Pennsylvania's Ben Franklin Partnership—The Promise of Technology.* Philadelphia: Commonwealth of Pennsylvania, 1987.

Robert J. Kopecek is president of Northampton County Area Community College in Bethlehem, Pennsylvania.

How can existing cooperative education programs be enhanced to achieve desired outcomes in work force development?

Renovating Cooperative Education Programs

Patricia A. Rheams, Fred Saint

Ongoing changes in technology, the economy, and the work force require different methods of educating and training workers. Cooperative education (co-op) programs can be an integral part of this endeavor. They can enhance recruitment and retention of target populations, help ensure that academic and training programs meet employer expectations, and provide for the immediate and long-term employability of graduates. To businesses, "Co-op can be an invaluable source . . . in achieving [employment and training] objectives" (American Association of State Colleges and Universities, 1988, p. 116). However, many colleges may be short-changing their students and communities by underutilizing co-op's potential (Waddell, 1990*b*).

This chapter identifies some work force development needs of the 1990s that can be met by community colleges through the use of co-op programs and suggests modifications of and enhancements to current co-op programs that are necessary to achieve desired work force and economic outcomes. For purposes of this chapter, we do not attempt to discuss the myriad, ancillary roles that co-op programs can play, such as serving as a center for contract education, industrial assessment, and academic credentialing. While some co-op programs may assume such roles, larger colleges are establishing specialized programs that, along with continuing education offices, can more specifically address those needs. For a further discussion of this broader view of cooperative education, James Varty's (1988) article "Cooperative Education for the 1990s and Beyond" is recommended.

NEW DIRECTIONS FOR COMMUNITY COLLEGES, no. 75, Fall 1991 © Jossey-Bass Inc., Publishers

Meeting the Work Force Crisis

The ability of a community to attract and retain viable employment sources for its citizens depends on many factors. As the manufacturing and agricultural sectors decline and information-based services increase, however, human resource factors become a prime concern. Is there an adequate trainable and retrainable labor force? Are reasonably priced training sources available?

The emerging labor force consists of populations that have traditionally sought opportunities at community colleges: minorities, immigrants, working adults, and women returning to the work force. In addition, emerging technologies require the type of training that community colleges can most quickly and easily develop (U.S. Department of Labor, 1989). However, the mere convergence of these two factors does not guarantee that community colleges will be able to purchase and house the variety of equipment necessary to train students in new technologies; that potential workers will seek the training at the community college; that once students, they will succeed and complete their programs; or that graduates will be readily and successfully employable.

According to the Hudson Institute's (1988) report for the U.S. Department of Labor, the work force in America will expand by only 1 percent annually in the 1990s, down from 2.9 percent in the 1970s. The number of workers in the age range of sixteen to twenty-four will drop by almost two million, or 8 percent. As the baby boom generation ages, the median age of the work force will climb from thirty-six, today, to thirty-nine by the year 2000. Women will comprise almost 66 percent of the new workers, blacks will make up 17 percent of the growth in the labor pool, and Hispanics will represent 29 percent of the total increase. Immigrants will make up the largest share of the increase in the work force. Of the twenty-one million jobs that will be created between now and the twenty-first century, almost 85 percent will be held by women, minorities, and immigrants (Johnston, 1987). Further, handicapped individuals are demanding accommodations that will enable them to be a productive segment of the work force. Although we may have survived in previous times without these workers in the labor pool, Carnevale and Gainer (1989, p. 50) suggest that "with the decline in the number of entry-level workers, the nation now needs all of its young people on the job to remain economically competitive." Some companies have already moved their operations overseas for lack of trained workers in this country. We *must* find more effective ways of recruiting, training, and retaining underutilized, "at-risk" populations.

As the population becomes even more heterogeneous, different learning styles and strategies become more important; and new competencies demand new learning environments. We can no longer rely on accumulating information because information continues to multiply. Students must learn practical ways to process information and function in life, organizations, and society. They must learn to be self-directed and to take responsibility for their own career development and learning, whether formal or informal. They must learn to make moral and ethical choices and to take responsibility for their actions. They must learn to take risks and overcome fear of failure in a "safe" atmosphere (R. Wilson, 1989). Co-op programs offer such learning environments.

The task of retraining the current work force offers special challenges. Workers no longer spend their entire careers with one employer. The U.S. Department of Labor estimates that by the year 2000 a worker will change careers three times and change jobs seven times. In fact, many large employers are offering extensive career counseling and educational benefits to encourage employees to prevent their own obsolescence. Often labor unions mandate such services in industries where downsizing is expected. However, it is not a quick or easy process to transform an undereducated work force into one capable of learning and relearning the new skills and competencies required in the high-technology information age. With technology advancing so rapidly, colleges may not be able to purchase or house the variety of equipment needed to make their graduates more marketable.

Although the community college is the logical provider of such training, it is often overlooked by both industry and workers. Employers naturally prefer to hire persons experienced in their equipment and systems and often get into bidding wars over them, thus driving up costs and prices. When experienced workers are not available and employers are willing to train, they often opt for short-term, specialized, in-house courses—sometimes at many times the price that the community colleges would charge. Displaced workers, as well as governmental agencies that refer them, tend to look for "quick fixes." This short-term training offers the hope of new employment in a quarter of the time that a two-year degree requires.

One company that is making an investment in the long-term development of its employees is Mitre Corporation in McLean, Virginia. Mitre offers an in-house A.A.S. degree program in business management through Northern Virginia Community College. Hoping to enroll 15 of its support staff, Mitre was overwhelmed when 110 expressed interest. With well-qualified support personnel in short supply, Mitre seized the opportunity to build employee loyalty while improving the basic and technical skills of its staff.

When training for a new career, workers experienced in one field often go through "reentry shock" when starting a new profession, exhibiting apprehension, lack of confidence, and disorientation in the new field. Additionally, Carnevale and Gainer (1989, p. 51) warn that "training outside the context of a job or job commitment is usually folly. Training does not create jobs. Jobs create the need for training."

Co-op programs can help solve these problems, and the benefits to be derived are numerous. Employers can be assured of a continuous flow of employees specifically trained in their equipment and systems by investing in potential workers while they are still in school, paying them entry-level salaries and observing their performance and potential before making a more permanent commitment. Because the trainees are pursuing a degree program, their basic skills and learning capacity are enhanced as they gain technical competence, thus maximizing their promotion potential. Colleges can expand their classrooms and laboratories into the employment community, utilizing the equipment and systems at all participating employer sites. Students can start working and earning in their respective fields after a minimum of related coursework, advancing in responsibilities and salaries as they progress in their studies. And with the structure and support of a formal co-op program, workers can ease their way into a new field while gaining confidence and the career development skills necessary for advancement.

What Is Cooperative Education?

Community colleges now represent 44 percent of all co-op programs in the United States. There are 437 co-op programs at community colleges throughout forty-seven states (J. Wilson, 1988). The community college movement blossomed at the same time that the U.S. Department of Education began providing seed money for the development of co-op programs on college campuses. The number of co-op programs has almost tripled since the early 1970s. In a way, these programs and community colleges have matured together.

Although each co-op program is unique, reflecting the college, student population, and employment base of the community, it is generally agreed that these academic programs combine classroom learning with practical, paid, progressive, on-the-job experience in the career field. Community college students usually earn both salaries and college credits based on the relevant learning that takes place on the job.

Co-op programs share aspects and benefits of other college programs and services, such as internships, college work/study, job placement, and credit for prior learning. But the combination of functions and responsibilities that makes co-op programs unique offers benefits that none of the other college programs can offer alone. While internships offer curriculum-related learning in a "real-world" setting, because the intern is temporary, employers generally do not invest in training of interns or delegate substantive, ongoing responsibilities to them, for example. Co-op programs, on the other hand, are meant to be ongoing and developmental, with new learning and responsibilities building on prior advances. True co-op programs have a *minimum* of two work terms, which may be consecutive on a full- or part-time basis, or alternating school and work terms. For the adult student, a full-time, continuing co-op assignment is often the most appropriate arrangement (American Association of Community and Junior Colleges, 1988).

Co-op Programs for Recruitment, Retention, and Technical Training

At the Alexandria Campus of Northern Virginia Community College (NOVA) the co-op program is used to recruit and retain career-change adults. Thousands of students have completed degree programs because they could see the relevance provided by their co-op jobs. Marginal students have found that they learn more effectively when they are able to apply what they learn in the classroom to a job situation. Career-change adults have found that co-op programs are the only sure way to enter competitive, new career fields (Waddell, 1990a).

In the Computer Information Systems (CIS) curriculum at NOVA, for example, two-thirds of the co-op students have prior bachelor's, master's, or Ph.D. degrees. Many were attracted to the campus because of the effectiveness of the co-op program. In recent years, up to 40 percent of the campus CIS graduates have been co-op students. Once we consider that at least 40 percent of the program-placed students are already working in the computer field and are not recruited for the co-op program, we can see that the program has greatly enhanced student recruitment and retention in the CIS curriculum.

The key ingredients have been to (1) structure the program in such a way and make it of sufficient duration that employers are motivated to invest in training and use the program as their primary recruitment source, (2) develop co-op positions that are so substantive that highly educated adults are challenged, (3) locate the positions in curricula with great professional potential and a dearth of entry-level opportunities, and (4) earn faculty support by showing how students are recruited and retained rather than lost because of their co-op participation (Waddell, 1990b, p. 25). Only because the experience has proven so essential and the value so great have career-change adults been willing to make substantial financial and personal sacrifices to get into and remain in the co-op program for a minimum of a year.

On a larger scale, LaGuardia Community College, Long Island, New York, has proven that long-term involvement in co-op programs pays off. At LaGuardia, each full-time student, whether enrolled in a transfer or occupational program, must complete three, three-month, full-time co-op assignments. LaGuardia has been the fastest-growing institution in New York State over the past fifteen years (Heinemann, 1988, p. 53).

Although traditional co-op policy has been to restrict program access to students who have already been successful in coursework, perhaps we should rethink that approach—especially if we are trying to attract and retain at-risk students. According to Carnevale and Gainer (1989, p. 50), "Preparing the disadvantaged for jobs with a future will require a mix of family support, basic education, and job training. Programs should be predicated on the principles that the best social welfare agency is a family, the best educator is experience, and the best trainer is a job."

Consider this: a "developmental-level" co-op component for students whose basic skills are being "developed" concurrently. By working closely with local unemployment and social service agencies, the community college could initially provide basic skills training through existing developmental programs and at the same time provide employment and life-skills training through a seminar and pre-co-op work experience phase (Waddell, 1990a). The objective would be to lay a firm foundation for planned career development while the student is still receiving public assistance, thus avoiding the trap of dead-end jobs that encourage workers to revert to public assistance. After the student has progressed to college-level coursework, he or she could make the transition into a "real" co-op position directly related to the career goal. With the continuing support of the co-op coordinator and co-op employer, the student can see progress being made toward a real career, not just a job. Because most community colleges are funded on the basis of Full-Time Equivalent enrollment (FTEs), the pre-co-op seminar and work experience course should be credit-bearing at the developmental level.

Many community colleges are involved with General Motors and Ford in programs that train automotive technology students on the companies' own equipment and systems, provide instructor training, and offer students one year of a co-op work experience in company dealerships. The federal government also has recently revised its co-op program, making it flexible enough to attract nontraditional students. Upon graduation, students may be noncompetitively converted to permanent positions. At NOVA the retention rate for computer students is 95 percent—a tribute to the quality of the co-op experience gained at the federal agencies.

Proposals

Based on anticipated human resource needs in the coming decade, the dramatic change in the demographic makeup of the emerging labor force, and the potential of community college co-op programs to help meet those needs and challenges, the following recommendations are offered: (1) Establish, expand, and strengthen co-op programs at community colleges along these lines: define co-op as a long-term, progressive experience with a minimum of two work periods (full-time, part-time, consecutive or alternating); direct efforts at placing students in new positions rather than validating existing work experience; emphasize learning and career development benefits rather than the use of credits toward graduation; and utilize co-op for career-change adults, displaced workers, and at-risk students. (2) Form partnerships with local employment and social service agencies to recruit at-risk students into programs that include co-op work experience. (3) Institute a developmental co-op for students who are not yet qualified for substantive co-op positions. (4) Utilize technology to share ideas and experiences, for example, the two-year college conference on the Cooperative Education Computer Network and teleconferencing. (5) Expand research in community college co-op programs, especially those effective with nontraditional students (Waddell, 1990b, p. 25).

A fully developed co-op program not only serves students and employers but the community and society as well. "Cooperative Education is the investment in which taxpayers not only reap an immediate dividend in student income taxes, but which pays a continuing annuity in terms of self-sufficient, higher earning citizens who truly earned a future when they earned a degree" (Rheams, 1985, p. 2). By building and renovating effective co-op programs, we can make a significant contribution to our investment in the future through work force and economic development.

References

American Association of Community and Junior Colleges. *Building Communities: A Vision for a New Century.* A Report of the Commission on the Future of Community Colleges. Washington, D.C.: American Association of Community and Junior Colleges, 1988. 35 pp. (ED 293 578)

American Association of State Colleges and Universities. *Allies for Enterprise: Highlights of the 1987–88 National Conference on Higher Education and Economic Development.* Washington, D.C.: American Association of State Colleges and Universities, 1988. 141 pp. (ED 304 961)

Carnevale, A. P., and Gainer, L. J. *The Learning Enterprise.* Washington, D.C.: American Society for Training and Development, 1989. 61 pp. (ED 304 581)

Heinemann, H. N. "Cooperative Education in the Community College." *Journal of Cooperative Education,* 1988, 24 (2–3), 53.

Hudson Institute. *Opportunity 2000.* Washington, D.C.: Government Printing Office, 1988.

Johnston, W. B. *Workforce 2000: Work and Workers for the 21st Century.* Indianapolis, Ind.: Hudson Institute, 1987. 143 pp. (ED 290 887)

Rheams, P. A. Testimony Before U.S. Congress, Senate Subcommittee on Education, Arts, and Humanities on the Reauthorization of Title VIII of the Higher Education Act. 99th Cong., 1st sess., 1985.

U.S. Department of Labor. *Investing in People: A Strategy to Address America's Workforce Crisis.* Washington, D.C.: Commission on Workforce Quality and Labor Market Efficiency, 1989. 71 pp. (ED 317 664)

Varty, J. "Cooperative Education for the 1990s and Beyond." *Journal of Cooperative Education,* 1988, 24 (2–3), 125–135.

Waddell, G. "Preparing Workers for Century 21." *Education Digest,* 1990a, 56 (4), 62–65.

Waddell, G. "Tips for Training a World-Class Work Force." *Community, Technical, and Junior College Journal,* 1990b, 60 (4), 21–27.

Wilson, J. *Cooperative Education in the United States and Canada.* Boston: Cooperative Education Research Center, Northeastern University, 1988.

Wilson, R. "Challenges of the 21st Century." Keynote address presented to the twenty-sixth annual conference of the Cooperative Education Association, Atlantic City, New Jersey, April 5, 1989.

Patricia A. Rheams is director, Cooperative Education, Alexandria Campus, Northern Virginia Community College, Alexandria, Virginia.

Fred Saint is instructional dean, Applied Sciences Institute, Montgomery Community College, Takoma Park Campus, Takoma Park, Maryland.

*The development of health care programs specific to community
needs can positively affect the supply of health services, provide
a stable work force since graduates of community colleges often
remain in the area, and increase accountability for programs.*

Meeting Health Care Credentialing Needs

Madeline K. Turkeltaub

Rapid expansion of health technologies has brought with it rapid change
in the expectations of those who work in this setting. Educational institutions must be prepared to be dynamic in order to produce the practitioners
who can function in the setting now and as it will be, rather than the way
it was! Trends related to the "graying of America" and increased use of
technology in health care settings have important curricular implications
(Waddell, 1990a).

Projections 2000 (U.S. Department of Labor, 1987) indicates that
expected growth in the health services between the years 1986 and 2000 is
third only to that of business and legal services. Health industry growth
will continue, with the largest number of job gains in physicians' offices,
nursing homes, and hospitals. Registered nursing is identified as the health
occupation with the most new jobs, projected at 612,000 from 1986 to
2000 (Personick, 1987).

The provision of practitioners who function well in the work setting is
an important step in gaining credibility, enhancing recruitment and retention of students in health care programs, and maintaining stability. The
economic impact on both the educational institutions and the employing
institutions is significant. Hospitals typically spend several thousands of
dollars per employee for orientation programs. Graduates who are not
properly prepared to function in the work setting may experience "reality
shock" from which they may not recover, resulting in high attrition and
loss of an employee in whom an investment has been made. Employers
also prefer to hire graduates from programs that have a good history of
success on credentialing examinations. The hiring of graduates of a nursing

program who do not pass the licensing examination for registered nurses again costs the employer an investment in time and money. Both of these situations reflect negatively on educational institutions, create a bad reputation in the respective communities, and result in decreased enrollments! Development of programs specific to the needs of a community will positively affect the supply of health care personnel in the area, provide a stable work force, and increase the accountability of the program to those it serves (Waddell, 1990b). This chapter examines challenges and opportunities for community colleges in health care credentialing.

Credentialing

Regulation within the health care community affects the success of college programs in a number of ways. The development of allied health programs is inextricably interrelated to the credentialing mechanisms of licensure, registration, certification, and accreditation. Although these terms are often used interchangeably, they are not necessarily synonymous. The interrelationships among credentialing mechanisms are complex. Often, the ability to become certified depends on the accreditation status of the program that was attended. The ability to take a licensure examination is dependent on whether the program has been improved by the licensing board. Admission of graduates into programs of higher education may be influenced by whether the original program of study was accredited by the appropriate professional accrediting body. Particular requirements of state departments of education and state boards for community colleges and general education and the interaction of governmental officials with professional regulatory bodies may at times make one feel as though the regulators were in conflict rather than working together to ensure high standards and protect the public. Efforts must be made to affect these interrelationships in positive ways. In Maryland, for example, all of the groups mentioned above worked together to design and implement a statewide articulation model for nursing education that allows direct transfer of college credits from licensed practical nursing programs to associate degree, registered nursing programs, and then to the baccalaureate degree in nursing. All relevant policies were developed with a team approach.

More than ever, as we look toward the twenty-first century, the need is evident for streamlining the system and working closely with all levels of educational institutions and employment agencies to provide a continuous flow of long-term health care providers. We cannot afford to waste health resources. The competencies of the graduate must be the same as the entry-level expectations of the employers. This match cannot be achieved in a vacuum. The professional organizations involved with developing licensing examinations, certification standards, and accreditation criteria must help to bridge the gap between education and practice. And the community college must carefully determine the extent of its commitment to developing and maintaining allied health programs since the investment in equipment and faculty is generally higher than is found in nonvocational programs.

Accreditation of Programs

The majority of allied health programs, other than nursing and dental-related programs, are accredited by the Committee on Allied Health Education and Accreditation of the American Medical Association (AMA). The AMA sponsors this activity and coordinates the needs of the medical profession with the allied health professional organizations. The twenty-six allied health professions involved in this process are listed in Exhibit 7.1.

A recent report of the AMA Division of Allied Health Education and Accreditation (Burrows and Hedrick, 1988, p. 1117) indicated that 130 more programs dropped their accreditation between 1983 and 1987 than were newly accredited. The major reason for withdrawal from the system was budgetary. The cost of the accreditation process includes not only the actual self-evaluation and associated costs for visitor expenses, secretarial support, and concentrated faculty time but also costs associated with compliance with essentials such as equipment, acceptable student-faculty ratios, and specific support services provided on campus.

Exhibit 7.1. Committee on Allied Health Education and Accreditation Health Programs

Anesthesiologist's assistant	Medical record technician
Cardiovascular technologist	Medical technologist
Cytotechnologist	Nuclear medicine technologist
Diagnostic medical sonographer	Occupational therapist
Electroneurodiagnostic technologist	Ophthalmic medical assistant
Emergency medical technician— paramedic	Profusionist
Histologic technician/technologist	Physician assistant
Medical assistant	Radiation therapy technologist
Medical illustrator	Radiographer
Medical laboratory technician (associate degree)	Respiratory therapist
	Respiratory therapy technician
Medical laboratory technician (certificate)	Specialist in blood bank technology
	Surgical assistant
Medical record administrator	Surgical technologist

Source: Burrows and Hedrick, 1988, p. 1114.

Nursing Programs as a Case in Point

Health careers provide excellent opportunities for community college students. The beginning salary for a registered nurse with an associate degree, exclusive of differential for shift and weekend hours, is among the highest for new community college graduates. Starting pay for new nurses in Maryland ranges from $23-27 thousand per year, exclusive of differential for weekend and shift work. The job security associated with health care careers is also a positive factor. The return to the community in terms of productive workers and taxes is great.

Nursing services can be viewed as a continuum of geriatric nursing assistants, medication aides, licensed practical nurses, registered nurses, and specialty nurses. Nursing curricula cannot be developed in isolation. Educators in nursing must constantly be aware of the interactions among the various levels of nursing education, since adequate nursing programs cannot be developed without a view of where the students have been and where they are going. Associate degree programs may act as a step on the career ladder for a licensed practical nurse to become a registered nurse and then to go on for a baccalaureate degree and beyond. A successful transition for the student within this system requires communication, cooperation, and coordination among the programs (subsystems) that constitute the whole system. Thus, the overall structure must be kept in mind when developing a curriculum, whether the term curriculum refers to a particular course, a group of nursing courses, or the entire nursing program. When analyzing the system, overall efficiency must be evaluated, and duplication of student effort must be minimized.

Nursing-related programs may involve both continuing education or noncredit courses and the courses taken for college credit. Most often the refresher programs for medication aide, geriatric aide, and registered nurse are offered through noncredit courses. The medication aide and geriatric aide courses lead to a certificate, which is required to function in those roles. The federal government recently specified the number of hours required for the training of a geriatric aide, and a nationally standardized certification examination is being developed. Medication aide programs provide certificates of completion, but there has been no standardized evaluation of the graduates. The certificate requirements create an opportunity for community colleges to develop partnerships with agencies, such as nursing homes, to provide these programs in a cost-effective manner. Certificate programs may also be conducted in vocational schools with health occupations programs. The trend toward standardization of certificate programs will assist in their acceptance as a step in the educational ladder toward nursing.

Portfolio development for nurses may also allow recognition of existing competencies and their relationship to continuing education efforts by nurses. Recruitment and retention of entry-level health care personnel is dependent to some degree on recognition of the knowledge and skills they attain. In the long term the community benefits from nurses' continued educational efforts since most nurses return the benefits in service to members of the community where they received the education.

Registered nurse education can be provided in hospital schools of nursing, four-year colleges and universities, or in community colleges. Associate degree programs for registered nurses produce more than 50 percent of new graduates each year. Nursing students must graduate from the programs in order to be eligible to take the licensing examination, thereby increasing the percentage of students who graduate. Approval is required for graduates to be eligible to take the licensing examination. Most boards of nursing require reports and periodic site visits to determine whether the programs are in compliance with federal rules and regulations. This type of external evaluation requires commitment on the part of the administration and faculty at each institution.

The American Nurses' Association and some specialty nursing organizations provide certification examinations for registered nurses that are not associated with degree requirements. Instead, the certification requirements include a specified number of years of practice in the specialty area, classes within a prescribed curriculum (such as those for certified critical care nurses), and successful completion of the specialty examination. Opportunities for partnerships and combined resources may include providing the prescribed program in cooperation with a health care agency or consortium of smaller organizations. Review courses in preparation for the certification examination can appropriately be provided by community colleges.

Moreover, registered nurse refresher courses are gradually being required for license renewal of inactive nurses by the boards of nursing in each state. Courses are approved by each board of nursing and are most often offered at local community colleges. Many states require continuing education prior to license renewal for registered nurses. This is a legal requirement.

Trends in the health care industry related to the graying of America, increased technology, home health care, and quality assurance define the direction of additional opportunities for new credit and noncredit programs at community colleges. For example, a 1989 federal law requiring credentialing of geriatric nursing assistants in nursing home settings has increased enrollments in programs that were previously voluntary. Since a nationally standardized examination is now mandatory, a reading level is expected that will allow one to function effectively in following medical prescription instructions, for example. The community college is the perfect setting for remedial courses in reading and writing that are necessary for passing the examination and functioning safely in the workplace.

When determining priorities in the selection of new programs, it is important to consider factors affecting student completion of the programs. Often, on-the-job training is provided to medical office assistants, home health aides, and dental assistants. Students, therefore, are not likely to complete a formal program, including general education courses, when they could be in the workplace earning the same salary with or without a credential. Consequently, when these education programs are tied to nursing or dental hygiene degree programs, an incentive for completion is created. The advantages of this approach for the student and for the college are great. Student time, effort, and potential are maximized, and the rate of student retention is increased. Health care employers are also satisfied because employees remain motivated within the system as they take advantage of educational opportunities, job satisfaction is enhanced, and retention is improved.

Conclusion

The explanation of the interaction of credentialing processes and higher education provided here for nursing services can be applied to many other allied health occupations. The partnerships between affiliate clinical agencies and the college, as well as between the college and other educational institutions, for the purpose of articulation of course requirements provide exciting opportunities for partnerships and shared resources that are clearly within the philosophy and mission of the community college. In order to improve articulation of courses and programs, share resources and reduce duplication of effort, it is important to (1) include representatives of employing agencies and local related organizations, such as the local dental society for dental assisting programs, on the program advisory committee; (2) constantly monitor the job market and be prepared to respond with the appropriate level of educational preparation to best meet the need; (3) utilize a ladder concept for educational mobility whenever starting a new program; (4) recognize where the students are coming from and where they hope to be going and then create appropriate paths of opportunity; (5) be aware of how the credential system relates to a specific program and consider the influence of mandatory versus voluntary credentialing on program completion; and (6) be flexible in program development.

The key to success is communication. Faculty and administrators responsible for noncredit courses must communicate with those responsible for credit courses on a regular basis. Representatives of the community college need to initiate dialogue with colleges and universities to provide further opportunities for articulation of programs and courses offered by four- and two-year institutions to avoid duplication of requirements in coursework and to ensure acceptance of community college credits by four-year institutions. By focusing on improved communication between credit and noncredit faculty and administrators in community colleges and continuing dialogue with four-year colleges and universities, students and educational institutions will benefit.

References

Burrows, W. R., and Hedrick, H. L. "Allied Health Education and Accreditation." *Journal of the American Medical Association,* 1988, *260* (8), 1113–1119.

Personick, V. "Industry Outlook in Employment Through the End of the Century." *Monthly Labor Review,* 1987, *110* (9), 30–45.

Waddell, G. "Preparing Workers for Century 21." *Education Digest,* 1990a, *56* (4), 62–65.

Waddell, G. "Tips for Training a World-Class Work Force." *Community, Technical, and Junior College Journal,* 1990b, *60* (4), 21–27.

Madeline K. Turkeltaub is director of the nursing program at Montgomery Community College, Montgomery County, Maryland, and is secretary of the Maryland Board of Nursing.

Telecourses are providing opportunities in the workplace for "lunchtime learning." Americans are sold on convenience, and distance learning is convenient.

Work Force Development Through Distance Learning

LaVerne W. Miller

The concept of learning at some distance from a source of teaching is not new. What is new are the developments in its evolution as new and different technologies have altered the methods of delivery while at the same time encompassing in the present what was useful in the past. Also new is the growth of distance learning in community colleges, which are using television, video, telephones, computers, and telecommunications devices to project learning programs into their communities. These new methods of course delivery have economic implications for the host institutions as well as for the communities that they serve.

The purpose here is to examine distance learning by telecourses, which is the form of distance learning most widely used in American community colleges. I include results of questionnaire responses from students at a community college over a ten-year period. These responses were used in determining student preferences and the reasons for them, which are important factors in understanding the audience to which telecourses appeal for marketing purposes.

In most community colleges, presentation of telecourses can be lucrative, especially when the colleges receive equivalent reimbursement of student hours from the state, similar to that for other credit courses. Each college assumes the responsibility for advertising and employing current faculty as instructors and staff to handle daily operations such as communicating with enrollees, sending out letters from instructors, and answering telephones.

Dedicated to democratic access to education, most large two-year colleges today have distance learning programs of one kind or another, depending on their locations and resources. The largest growth and use of distance learning in America, however, has been and remains in the offerings of public four-year institutions. Many of these were land grant colleges whose extension services originally served rural populations.

Outside the United States, in such large land-mass countries as Australia, Canada, China, and the Soviet Union, distance learning is essential to education because of the size, accessibility, or geography of the countries and the nature of their populations and educational institutions. As new technologies are added, there is no diminution of the skills required in older methods of delivery, but rather an inclusion of them as the technologies develop.

Despite the addition of technologies such as satellite broadcasting and interactive video and computers, the new medium of telecommunications still encompasses the old medium. The implication of this notion is that although the electronic media are trying to push us into new phases of development, they still depend on student mastery of the old skills. The student must know how to read and write regardless of the medium he or she is using.

Use and Convenience of New Technologies

Zigerell (1984) provides one of the best definitive descriptions of the national and international use of new technologies in distance learning. His book is state of the art, with a useful bibliography and glossary of terms, and is highly recommended.

Given that most U.S. residents live within reasonably close proximity to a two- or four-year college, there might appear to be little need for distance learning or telecourses. However, Americans are sold on convenience, and distance learning is a convenient way to pursue education in both rural and urban areas. Distance education is like a convenience store—available at a wide variety of hours at the most accessible of locations. Registering and paying are easy, driven only by the student's own motivation.

A 1989 survey of Howard Community College's telecourse students confirms that convenience is a factor in many students' decisions to participate in this form of learning (Livieratos, 1989). Of the students who enrolled in telecourses during the 1989 academic year, over 70 percent indicated that they lacked the time for class attendance, and nearly that many saw telecourses as a way of combining school with family responsibilities. Over half indicated that they enrolled in the telecourses to minimize travel.

The Instructional Television Consortium's 1986 *Telecourse Utilization Survey* provides a wealth of information on community colleges that are using telecourses (Brey, 1988). The report can be used to identify those colleges using a particular telecourse or delivery system and those willing to share telecourses originally produced for their own use. Of the 181 telecourses identified by the survey, many have applications for work force development, including courses in accounting, basic electronics, business management, how to start a small business, marketing, office procedures, programming and systems performance, and a variety of communications skills. The most frequently offered course, "The Business File," was used 121 times, with an average enrollment of thirty-nine students.

Montgomery Community College Survey

What is the market for such telecourses? Responses to a questionnaire administered to telecourse students at Montgomery Community College in Maryland over the ten-year period between 1979 and 1989 show that the target population did not change significantly over that decade. Sixty to seventy percent were female. The average age of twenty-nine in 1984 had advanced to thirty by 1987 and stayed there through spring 1989. Less than 1 percent of the students were over sixty years of age. The largest groups were initially between the ages of eighteen and thirty-five, but in the last year of the survey more students fell in the thirty-six to forty-six age range. Some students who continued to take telecourses may have contributed to the age increase by being in the program several years. One could ask, then, whether the same students are "hooked" on telecourses and continue to take them. In general, the target population may be self-selecting; that is, telecourses might be the preferred learning style of those who choose them.

Community college telecourses appear to appeal to the age group of eighteen to forty and to those who want upward mobility. Responses to the question about the most important reasons to enroll in a telecourse reveal that 73-75 percent were taking courses in order to obtain a degree; the next most popular reason was improvement or advancement; and the lowest was for general interest. Students believe that degrees lead to new job opportunities or on-the-job upgrading, which mean occupational advancement and more money.

A large proportion of students own videocassette recorders and tape the programs. However, for those who do not own this equipment, a learning lab may be needed as a place for viewing the off-air tapes. Typically, copyright permission is granted by the broadcast station and paid for through a per-student fee levied by the station.

Students in the Montgomery Community College study described themselves as largely professional or office workers. There were a few (less than 1 percent) older students who were retired and did not want or need course credits. They came to the college to get away from home, interact with others, and have fun taking courses in art, physical education, and so forth.

Students in this study were predominantly white. They were registered at an urban campus where approximately one-third of the population is composed of non-native speakers, including many Asians and Hispanics.

When an institution is contemplating presentation of telecourses, it is useful to know that most telecourse students are daytime workers who mostly prefer Saturdays and Sundays as viewing days, and either end of the day, late evening or early morning, as their viewing hours—factors important in programming. A group of courses also can be offered at noon, another favorite time when presented at the workplace. At work students can watch courses on topics such as management, marketing, psychology, accounting, or language, grouped under the rubric of "lunchtime learning." These courses can be offered at other times as well for the convenience of those who cannot participate at work.

The numbers in the "not currently employed" group of the Montgomery Community College survey remained steady (around 10 percent) except for 1986, when the number rose to 13 percent from 6 percent the previous semester. (Some students who reported being unemployed may be homemakers who do not work outside their homes.) This datum is relevant because the demand for workers in the Montgomery County area has been and remains very strong, especially in the health, clerical, and service fields. Shopping malls advertise for help frequently. Like students on campus, telecourse students each semester have been predominantly and consistently part-time (ranging from 67 to 70 percent); full-time student enrollments remained constant, and students increasingly took other courses on the campuses, along with their telecourses, especially at night. Ninety to ninety-five percent of telecourse students enrolled between 1984 and 1989 said that they had taken a regular on-campus class at Montgomery Community College or at some other college. Five to seven percent had completed work beyond the baccalaureate degree. These findings indicate that the telecourse populations are not new to college and that the program is tapping the edge of a market that contains former college students who are either refurbishing work skills, such as in business courses, or are attempting to fulfill their humanities or social sciences degree requirements.

At Montgomery Community College, we have long claimed that television courses can generate on-site students for the campuses. Fifty-five to fifty-seven percent of the students in this study said that they planned to enroll in regular on-campus classes. The telecourses, in this sense, could be thought of as a marketing tool for the campus classes.

Part of the folklore of instructional television deals with the lure of distance learning and the inability of some students to get to the college campus. In this study, students said that they could have gone to the campus but they did not want to go. Hence, they had other reasons for taking distance learning courses. As previously indicated, the data show that the single most important reason for taking telecourses was to earn credits toward a college degree. Second was the need for professional improvement or advancement, and last was general interest. The most important reasons, then, suggest the belief that a degree will earn one more status or money, as will professional improvement or advancement, and telecourses are a means to the end of increased status or earnings. This is a vital aspect in promotion of the courses. General or cultural interest remains, but not at the same level as the projected material gain.

We have also assumed that telecourses appeal particularly to students who have difficulty in coming to the campus because of handicaps. In this study only an infinitesimal number of telecourse students (1 percent or less) had a handicap. The responses over the decade show that an increasing number of students had transportation available to them. Thus, promotion of telecourses in terms of student transportation problems is at odds with the study's findings.

In a comparison of five years (1984–1989) at Montgomery Community College, consistent patterns appeared that provide useful information in attracting students and may be of special interest to new telecourse users. In all semesters the most often cited ways of learning about television courses were (1) through the class schedule, (2) through the telecourse brochure, which evening students from previous semesters receive in the mail, (3) through brochures picked up at the college (for example, library circulation desks and counseling offices) or elsewhere, and (4) through friends. The least influence was generated by newspaper advertisements.

One of the most disappointing aspects of the responses to the questionnaire was the small part played by the college counselors in suggesting telecourses to students. The reasons that they do not direct more students to telecourses need to be investigated further.

Conclusion

The students who participated in the Montgomery Community College study were not unusual. Hence, it can be assumed that in the approximately fifteen hundred colleges nationwide where credit is given for courses through the Public Broadcasting System's Adult Learning Services, most people are attracted to community college programs because of their convenience, not because of student distance from a site.

Although few community colleges offer enough distance learning courses for a degree, students, in most states, can transfer telecourse credits to other community colleges in the state telecourse consortia and to the state universities. During periods of belt-tightening and increasingly fewer options among on-campus courses, telecourses offer an alternative when the on-campus classes that students want are unavailable or are canceled because of low, on-campus enrollments.

As we move toward the one hundredth anniversary of distance learning, we are seduced by the new technological variations on the theme and their nationwide and international implications. We are concerned about the cost-effectiveness of the new technologies, which are, in the case of computers, developing more rapidly month-by-month than one can keep up with—smaller, faster, cheaper! As the technology becomes more complicated, will it increasingly confuse students or enchant them? Will it "turn off" the students who want simpler learning devices? It will be important to carefully consider each new technology and its applicability versus its complexity. Will it work dependably? Does it add something so substantial that it is worth the complexity and the cost?

Community colleges benefit financially from telecourses, so they are worth marketing in terms of dollar return. It has been possible at one community college, by penurious management and good investments, to build a surplus of $500,000. Distance learning courses must be accepted by the college faculty and community to be academically viable, however, and this struggle is continuing.

At the core, regardless of the medium, there must be relevant content and the appropriate student skills to apply to the content, especially reading, writing, and self-discipline. Successful students are skilled and highly motivated achievers. Motivation is the energizing force behind and the key to all successful distance learning. It is for the student who has goals and literacy skills and can organize his or her time and set personal objectives. Distance learning at the community college is not for everyone. For some, however, it is a convenient service of education. Those who want to learn from a distance do so, and they apply what they learn in the workplace. And they often improve their own economic conditions as a result of the learning and practice.

References

Brey, R. *Telecourse Utilization Survey, First Annual Report: 1986–1987 Academic Year.* Washington, D.C.: American Association of Community and Junior Colleges, Instructional Television Consortium, 1988. 86 pp. (ED 301 295)

Livieratos, B. B. *Distance Learners: Howard Community College's Fiscal Year 1989 Telecourse Students.* Columbia, Md.: Howard Community College, 1989. 35 pp. (ED 311 980)

Zigerell, J. *Distance Education: An Information Age Approach to Adult Education.* Columbus, Ohio: ERIC Clearinghouse on Adult, Career, and Vocational Education, 1984. 84 pp. (ED 246 311)

LaVerne W. Miller is professor and director of Special Instructional Services at Montgomery Community College, Takoma Park Campus, Montgomery County, Maryland.

The American community college concept has been exported to several countries, although the basic concept has originated independently in various forms worldwide. Now we are seeing opportunities to import these conceptual variations from other countries, allowing us to improve our own system.

Exporting the Community College Concept: Worldwide Variations

Joseph Arthur Greenberg

Uniquely American in the details of concept and design, community colleges are distinct in diversity and adaptability as well as in responsiveness to societal needs. The scope and variety of programs, coupled with the emphasis on student services and compensatory education, set community colleges apart from other types of educational institutions. As Cohen and Brawer (1989, p. 357) suggest, "The community college is a system for individuals, and it does what the best educational forms have always done: It helps individuals learn what they need to know to be effective, responsible members of their society." Two-year public colleges were developed in response to several social forces, including the need for trained workers for America's growing and expanding industries, the lengthened period of adolescence, and the drive for social equality (Cohen and Brawer, 1989). Their growth and development were also influenced by a national desire for equal opportunity in and access to postsecondary education.

Currently, there are 1,088 public community colleges, enrolling over 4,700,000 students and employing more than 250,000 faculty (El-Khawas, Carter, and Ottinger, 1988). American community colleges possess distinct qualities developed during the remarkable growth period in the middle of this century (Eaton, 1988) and now constitute the largest single block of higher education institutions in the United States (Paradise, 1988).

Exporting an Idea

As most nations throughout the world continue to experience increases in the demand for postsecondary education, the American community college has gained considerable attention (Kintzer, 1979). By request, we have exported the community college concept to several nations and have observed its influence on many others. Most countries have adapted the concept to fit their individual goals and objectives, resulting in various forms of the American-style community college.

Currently, twelve countries are associate members of the American Association of Community and Junior Colleges (Jones, 1989). Among these twelve countries, there are thirty-one separate institutions holding membership. In addition, many other countries have incorporated some form of the American community college into their educational systems. For example, two years ago the United Arab Emirates began a system of fourteen two-year colleges, two in each of the seven emirates. The colleges focus on career education and provide opportunities for university transfer. Indonesia has been interested in the community college concept for some time and has initiated relationships with several American two-year colleges. The Indonesian Pesantren (informal community schools) movement has gained great popularity and appears to incorporate several elements of the American system. The Indonesian Inter-Islamic University Council, representing more than 150 Islamic universities, has expressed interest in adapting a two-year community-type institution to its university system. The lack of economic support, however, has prevented this from occurring.

The Scandinavians call the community-type institution "folkhighschool," the Brazilians refer to it as "SENAI," Yugoslavians have "higher schools," and the Japanese have "junior colleges." Whatever the name, the influence of the American community college concept is apparent in the international setting and spreads as countries attempt to meet the emerging employment and community service needs of their populations. The exportation of the community college concept will continue, and, in turn, American community colleges will be influenced by the growth and development of systems in other countries.

Gilliland (1986) compares Danish folkhighschools and American community colleges, describing several folkhighschools and stressing the value of tours abroad by American educators. Characteristics of folkhighschools include open-door policies, a broad range of social strata and ages in the student body, absence of formal diplomas and examinations, and curricula based on cultural and social problems.

Adapting the Concept Internationally

Internationalization of the community college concept reflects the diversity that is the hallmark of the American community college. Four separate adaptations of the American system are as follows:

Canadian Community Colleges. Community colleges in Canada are "characterized by diversity with respect to their relations with the government, the scope and range of their programs, and the ways in which they respond to societal needs" (Dennison and Levin, 1988, p. 49). The colleges all share a commitment to providing access to a wide range of individuals who need educational opportunities beyond secondary school. According to Dennison (1980), Canadian community colleges have experienced a rapid growth in numbers of students and new schools. These colleges have the following essential characteristics: (1) broadly comprehensive curricula, including various combinations of academic, university transfer, technical/ career, vocational, basic adult upgrading, and remedial courses, as well as community education programs, (2) a commitment to quality teaching and broad-based student counseling, (3) an open admissions policy, (4) minimum tuition fees, (5) course scheduling in nontraditional time slots to accommodate student needs, and (6) responsiveness to the community in policy-making, program development, and student characteristics.

These descriptions of essential characteristics could be placed in almost any American community college catalog, and although there are a few fundamental differences between the two systems (for example, funding formats and governmental relationships), the similarities are overwhelming. In addition to experiencing massive periods of growth and identical characteristics, Canadian and American community colleges are guided also by general principles that can be applied to colleges and systems in each country. Dennison and Levin (1988) indicate that these principles have contributed to the development of community colleges in all provinces and regions of Canada. These common principles can be expressed as follows: (1) The community college is designed to provide access to educational opportunity for societal groups previously denied such access through the imposition of academic, socioeconomic, geographical, and cultural barriers. (2) The community college must maintain a comprehensive curricular model that provides for both education and training within a broad range of program offerings. (3) Community colleges are designed to emphasize student orientation through the priority given to faculty instruction, faculty-student contact, and accessible and comprehensive counseling services. (4) Community colleges must maintain a community orientation through their governance and program advisory structures. And (5) community colleges must adapt to changes in external phenomena such as new student clienteles, demand for programs of training and education, technological changes, and changes in program delivery and structure of the workplace.

Canadian community colleges are confronted with problems and issues that bear a striking resemblance to the problems and issues facing American community colleges. Canadian institutions have coped with budgetary constraints during the last several years and are being asked for increased accountability. In addition, strained relations with federal and state governments and the impact of collective bargaining have led these colleges to focus on the task of developing solutions to these extremely complex problems (Dennison, 1985). Given these problems, Dennison and Levin (1988) suggest that Canadian community colleges will be hard-pressed in continuing to emphasize their traditional functions.

Dennison and Levin (1988) present the results of a study of Canadian community college goals as perceived by their chief executive officers and the provincial personnel responsible for college development. The study reveals continued emphasis on early development goals and goals reflecting provincial differences in priorities. In general, the results show diversity in community college roles and contributions.

German/Austrian Volkshochschule. The German/Austrian Volkshochschule (VHS) is the Western European counterpart of the American community college. Literally, it is the "peoples' higher school." One of the central missions of the VHS is to promote the "socialization" of its constituents, and it has assumed a significant leadership posture in this regard in most of the communities that it serves. The main similarity between the American community college and the VHS is their leadership roles in developing and achieving community goals.

Several community college/VHS comparisons are possible, including number of institutions, enrollment, admissions, costs, programs, facilities, governance, organization, and finance. The following comparisons are especially noteworthy:

1. Both the community college and the VHS enroll well over four million "participants" (the VHS term for students).

2. By law, various German "lands" or states were committed to the support of universal, public education. The major vehicle to fulfill this legal pledge is the network of VHSs. VHSs are public centers and as such are available to those who are motivated to take part in their programs. Of course, this is similar to the American community college "open-door" commitment.

3. This ideal of open access is further promoted by both institutions in the form of low or moderate tuition and fees. Costs remain reasonable in relation to the economy, as they do in U.S. two-year colleges.

4. The two major curricular thrusts in the VHS parallel those found in the developmental/remedial and community services/noncredit areas of the U.S. community college.

5. Most VHSs do not have their own buildings or campuses but instead tend to be institutions without walls, renting or leasing space in other schools. A very small number of VHSs have their own buildings (or *haus*). Where this is the case, the building is usually provided by the local town or city government, and it is frequently shared with the local library.

6. In general, German and Austrian VHSs are operated by a public dues-paying "association" of local citizenry. The association is composed of an annually elected executive committee or board of directors that governs the financial affairs of the VHS. A second, larger committee or board

is made up of VHS instructors, staff, other educators, and citizens. This board is charged with approving the VHS program and course offerings.

7. The VHS organizational patterns resemble the American community colleges "without walls." That is, they have a full-time chief executive officer and several full-time departmental chairs who organize the classes and screen and hire instructors to teach departmental courses. Classes are almost always taught by part-time instructors recruited from the community served by the VHS. One frequent criticism is the lack of full-time faculty and the stabilizing influence such a group of professionals can provide.

8. The final comparison, finance, is similar to the extant patterns of the American community college. Revenue to operate most VHSs is provided by the federal (Bonn) government, by local governments in the local VHS service area, and by the participants and students. The two largest sources of support are state and local governments. The federal contribution is decreasing, as it is in the United States, and participants are often called on to make up the difference with higher class fees.

While VHS and American leadership arenas are similar, the VHS leadership objectives tend to be less tangible and more social than are those of most American community colleges. Community colleges appear to formally recognize and champion programmatic goals; in contrast, the VHS officially publicizes itself in terms of societal and cultural goals and objectives (Bogart, 1985). The stated leadership objective of the American community college is to provide a flexible, community-based, educational program that is responsive to the perceived needs of local businesses and industry, as well as to the needs of its individual constituents. American community colleges attempt to respond to national priorities and issues as they filter into and affect their communities.

Bogart (1985) draws comparisons between the German VHS and the American community college. After highlighting the mission of the VHS in promoting the socialization of its constituents, he contrasts VHSs and community colleges in terms of enrollment, admissions, costs, programs, facilities, governance, organization, and finance. Emphasis is placed on the open access provided by the VHS, its low student costs, its provision of special interest courses, the existence of a degree comparable to the associate degree, and the provision of funding for the VHS by federal, state, and local governments.

Brazil and the SENAI. Kempner (1986) provides a comparison of Brazil's education of its emerging middle class with the U.S. community colleges' education of their constituencies. He correctly asserts that the United States tends to compare the rest of the world's educational system with its own, but when viewed through the lens of comparative education, escape from such parochialism is possible given the differing educational realities. This viewpoint also relates to the cases of Canadian community colleges and the German/Austrian VHS. Comparative education can serve as a vehicle for critical assessment and enables an evaluation of the relative merits of one system within its unique cultural context with respect to the merits of other systems.

Brazil has a distinct, two-tiered educational system consisting of private and public schooling, a lack of universal secondary schooling, and limited access to postsecondary education through the public school system. While the private system offers a well-structured educational hierarchy, the public system has great gaps in the middle of its structure, supported by a weak base (Kempner, 1986). One solution, although narrow (Castro, 1986), to the problem of closing the gap in the middle of Brazil's public educational structure for the lower-middle and working classes is a private educational enterprise called SENAI. The major objectives of SENAI are (1) to find new and better ways to provide a sound general education on which to build the specific education related to a trade, (2) to develop the individual potential of its students, and (3) to help those enrolled in its vocational training centers fill useful roles in society (Andrade, Silva, and Abreu, 1984).

SENAI has six national training institutes and a network of vocational training centers. Students are allowed to enter SENAI only upon completion of at least four years of education. SENAI's curriculum is devoted to the specific training needs of industry, and it appears to excel in teaching the appropriate technical skills needed on the job.

According to Kempner (1986), in Brazil no institution directly comparable to the American community college exists. SENAI, as discussed, offers educational opportunities to a unique and small segment of the working class and is not a postsecondary institution in the same manner as is the community college. Regardless of the narrowness of the SENAI solution, SENAI offers a potential similar to that of the American community college. How this potential can be realized is a task for educators and politicians. Both SENAI and the community college offer unique educational opportunities to the lower-middle levels of their respective societies, yet neither effectively offers education to those at the very bottom of the social structure. SENAI does provide, however, an innovative educational system that can assist both countries in the task of determining how to provide educational opportunities to the lowest social class.

Kempner (1986) compares Brazil's education of its emerging middle class with the U.S. community colleges' education of their middle- and lower-class constituencies. First, Kempner argues that just as there are stratified technological levels within the labor market, levels of knowledge can also be distinguished. Specifically, access to high-status knowledge is a critical problem in determining the equity of a nation's educational system. After presenting a rationale for comparing the two educational systems, Kempner defines "middle class" for the purposes of the analysis, examines Brazil's two-tiered educational system of public and private schooling, and describes SENAI as a private educational enterprise offering industry-oriented vocational training to a select group of working-class students. Next, the U.S. community colleges are described and assessed in terms of how well they serve the educational needs of the middle and lower classes. Educational innovations that have been implemented in Brazil with limited success are also reviewed, including efforts to offer a two-year postsecondary curriculum and to expand access to the university through night classes. Kempner concludes that both SENAI and the community college offer unique educations to the lower-middle levels of their respective societies, yet neither effectively offers education for those at the very bottom of the social structure.

Iran: A Proposed Two-Year Comprehensive Community College Model for Developing Nations. The prior sections describing Canada, Germany, and Brazil represent real examples of community college adaptations. Here, I focus on a proposal (Abili, 1988) for a two-year comprehensive community college model for developing nations, using Iran as a case in point. Abili (1988) recommends adopting the comprehensive community college model, with certain modifications, in order to contribute to the solution of Iran's local, regional, and national middle-level employment problems and to meet the educational and occupational expectations of Iranian youth.

The American-style community college seems appropriate for the following reasons: (1) Because of massive destruction resulting from the war with Iraq, candidates for Iran's current and future job market require technical and scientific knowledge, generally unavailable in Iran's educational programs. (2) Population growth and economic changes require Iran to develop new institutions providing new areas of training. (3) Current economic pressures require development of special postsecondary institutions offering "short-cycle" (Kintzer, 1979) education and training that are not currently available in the university. And (4) the majority of Iranian high school seniors attend the nearest college to home, but they have indicated that they would attend a two-year postsecondary institution with transfer and job-training programs.

The proposed community college model for Iran, as an alternative to the nation's present postsecondary institutions, is designed to fulfill Iran's educational and work force needs. The model is presented in three components: (1) admissions policy, (2) control and finance, and (3) comprehensiveness.

Abili provides an overview of Iran's current economic status and needs, the advantages that the development of a community college system would afford the country, the specific educational needs that could be met by a two-year postsecondary educational system, and the steps that need to be taken to ensure the success of the institutions. After presenting the components of the proposed model, he then presents recommendations concerning the programs that should be offered by the institutions, including transfer, adult education, agriculture education, teacher training, general education, remedial education, and guidance and counseling. Abili stresses the need to consider the values of the Iranian people, local customs and traditions, patterns of interaction, and indigenous academic traditions in implementing the community college model in Iran.

Conclusion

The American-style community college concept is a truly unique idea and will continue to be used in full or in part by those nations interested in alternative approaches to meeting societal demands. An examination of the various adaptations of the original American concept reveals lessons about structure and finance for all countries and provides direction for improving certain functions of each institutional form.

The Brazilian SENAI represents creative and practical strategies for educating the emerging middle class in order to meet the demands of these individuals and of the Brazilian economy. The use of quality circles as a participative management technique in Japanese junior colleges has already been adopted by several American community colleges (Ruff, 1984), and the German VHS holds firmly to its mission of promoting the socialization of its constituency through a filter of morality, values, and culture (a success that led Bogart [1985] to plead with American community colleges to recognize and promote such socialization).

These examples and many others suggest the need for additional research on successful programs and designs and on how they can be applied in other countries and cultures. AACJC maintains a list of international associate members and possesses several reports and papers relating to international community colleges and alternative institutions. These and other resources (for example, ERIC and DATRIX) can help us to expand the knowledge base about current practices. With this knowledge base we can better access new ideas for making community colleges and similar institutions more efficient and effective and thus contribute to the improvement of peoples and communities.

References

Abili, K. "A Two-Year Comprehensive Community College Model for Developing Nations: A Case of Iran." Unpublished manuscript based on doctoral dissertation, Department of Education, University of Michigan, 1988. 22 pp. (ED 291 419)

Andrade, A. F., Silva, E. R., and Abreu, F. J. "Evaluation of Current Vocational Training in Progress in Brazil." In G. Schachter (ed.), *Brazil Vocational Education: Aspects of Economic Policy and Planning.* Boston: Northeastern University Center for Higher Education, 1984.

Bogart, Q. J. "The Community College and the Volkshochschule: An International

Comparison of Leadership Objectives in the Adult Teaching/Learning Process."
Paper presented at the sixty-fifth annual national convention of the American
Association of Community and Junior Colleges, San Diego, California, April
1985. 12 pp. (ED 225 261)

Castro, C. M. "Educating the Emerging Middle Class in Brazil." In K. Kempner,
paper presented at the sixty-seventh annual conference of the American Educational Research Association, San Francisco, Calif., April 1986.

Cohen, A. M., and Brawer, F. B. The American Community College. (2nd ed.) San
Francisco: Jossey-Bass, 1989.

Dennison, J. D. "The Community College in Canada—An Educational Innovation."
Unpublished manuscript, Department of Education, University of British Columbia, Vancouver, 1980. 31 pp. (ED 226 778)

Dennison, J. D. "Community Colleges in Canada: Future Issues, Future Solutions."
Unpublished manuscript, Department of Education, University of British Columbia, Vancouver, 1985. 26 pp. (ED 276 461)

Dennison, J. D., and Levin, J. S. "Goals of Community Colleges in Canada: A 1987
Perspective." Canadian Journal of Higher Education, 1988, 18 (1), 49–63.

Eaton, J. S. Colleges of Choice: The Enabling Impact of the Community College. New
York: Macmillan, 1988.

El-Khawas, E., Carter, D. J., and Ottinger, C. A. The Community College Fact Book.
New York: American Council on Education/Macmillan, 1988.

Gilliland, J. R. "Folkhighschool: The People's College of Scandinavia." Community,
Junior, and Technical College Journal, 1986, 56 (5), 22–25.

Jones, E. B. A Report on the Minority Business Enterprise Project, 1983–1989. Washington, D.C.: American Association of Community and Junior Colleges, 1989.

Kempner, K. "Educating the Emerging Middle Class in Brazil: A Comparative Analysis of SENAI and the American Community College." Paper presented at the
sixty-seventh annual conference of the American Educational Research Association, San Francisco, April 1986. 15 pp. (ED 272 243)

Kintzer, F. C. "World Adaptations of the Community College Concept." In M. C.
King and R. I. Breuder (eds.), Advancing International Education. New Directions
for Community Colleges, no. 26. San Francisco: Jossey-Bass, 1979.

Paradise, M. E. "United States Community Colleges." Unpublished manuscript,
American Association of Community and Junior Colleges, Washington, D.C.,
1988.

Ruff, D. "Laying the Groundwork for the Effective Implementation of Quality Circles
in a Community College." Paper presented at the twenty-fourth annual forum of
the Association for Institutional Research, Fort Worth, Texas, May 1984. 33 pp.
(ED 287 525)

Joseph Arthur Greenberg is professor of higher education administration at
George Washington University, Washington, D.C., and has served as a consultant
in community and junior college education in Indonesia and Korea.

How can community colleges assist businesses with trading in a global economy? What obstacles do businesses and community colleges face in seeking out world trade opportunities?

Trading in a Global Economy: Obstacles and Opportunities

Robert L. Gell, James A. Crupi

After experiencing one success in the export arena, an executive of a major East Coast lumber company has all but given up hope of ever again participating in international trade. He explained that he frequently receives requests to bid on lumber contracts in Europe, but because the specifications are stated in metric measurements, he is compelled to convert them into inches and feet since his equipment is set to saw boards in U.S. units of measure. The thought of using a metric scale on his saws seems un-American to him, and, needless to say, he has never received a response to his bids. This experience illustrates a lack of appreciation of the basic elements of the world economy and of world trade.

A manufacturer of specialty wire explained that even though open to offers from international firms, the company was currently at capacity supplying the domestic market, and that as long as their account managers made enough calls on customers, the firm would prosper. When asked about their efforts in the international marketplace, the response was that price lists are sent to anyone requesting them. Prices are in U.S. dollars and are reviewed once each year. Neither recognition nor appreciation of the fluctuation of the dollar vis-à-vis foreign currency was apparent. The fact that significant discounts are often available to firms quoting prices in local currency was not known by the chief executive officer. The same firm was expecting a delegation of Japanese business representatives later in the afternoon. Their arrival time was not known since they were coming by taxi. There was no appreciation of the common custom among international firms of providing limousine service for visiting business representatives. Absent among many business executives and public officials is a

NEW DIRECTIONS FOR COMMUNITY COLLEGES, no. 75, Fall 1991 © Jossey-Bass Inc., Publishers

knowledge of proper protocol for entertaining and welcoming international business representatives. Many times politicians offend international visitors and create a climate that is less than conducive to good trade relations. While many Americans are comfortable with transactions with Europeans, few feel completely comfortable entertaining oriental, Mid-Eastern, and other international business representatives.

A firm that manufactures elements for office equipment had a rude educational experience in the field of international competition when a Japanese manufacturer that previously had marketed only its equipment began to also provide parts and service. Overnight a part that the American manufacturer had been making and marketing for $25 was made available by the Japanese manufacturer for $15. Companies with executives who believe that their future is firmly established in the domestic market do not realize that an entire product line could be eliminated without warning.

Reading today's headlines, we soon realize that the world is changing, but few of us understand what impact these changes will have on us. Many of us take comfort in the glories of the past and blindly believe that regardless of what happens in the rest of the world, our country will remain strong and economically sound. The fact is that time is running out. And unless we can turn around our current slide in the world economy, the lives of our children will be extremely different from our own. If American values and thinking are reflected in our national product advertising, we should be extremely concerned when Buick claims proudly that its automobile has the best service record of an "American-made" car, as though foreign cars either do not exist or are not important. Do General Motors executives actually believe that their only competition is in the United States?

In the 1980s, 70 percent of American industries were competing with foreign businesses (Luke, Ventriss, Reed, and Reed, 1988). For example, foreign competitors had captured 90 percent of the U.S. cutlery market, 30 percent of the machine tools market, and over 20 percent of the steel market (Luke, Ventriss, Reed, and Reed, 1988, p. 113). America's share of world exports in manufacturing dropped to 17 percent in 1985. Since 1981, "over two and one-half million jobs have been lost to foreign competition. One out of eight U.S. jobs in manufacturing is tied to exports and one-third of U.S. corporate profits are derived from international business activities" (Kline, 1984, p. 82). It is not surprising that "U.S. companies are shifting their production overseas to take advantage of lower costs" (Luke, Ventriss, Reed, and Reed, 1988, p. 113). At the same time, an increase in foreign investments in U.S. business enterprises is evident. Could this explain why states and communities are developing strategies to respond to a global economy?

Participants at the National Governors' Association (1987) declared that the "key to prosperity is the global view" and issued a report that "emphasized steps necessary to improve America's competitive economic position" (Gleazer, 1989, p. 139). The report asserted that states and localities "must maintain an international perspective in all decisions, ranging from how we market our goods to how we educate our children." A recommended area of action by states was "helping local communities tailor their economies to global realities" (National Governors' Association, 1987). Community colleges may be especially interested in following up on this recommendation in light of the questions raised here.

These global realities, along with common knowledge, tell us that most of the firms that are not serving international markets will be out of business ten years from now. Little in our community can escape the reality of the international marketplace. While our communities are endowed with talented leaders in both the private and public sectors, they have not been, nor are they currently being, adequately trained to face an internationally competitive world. Most do not see a global market and do not understand how to engage it. The challenge then is to expand the global vision of our business people so that their arena in which to buy, sell, train, and create relationships grows as well.

With few exceptions, most business, political, academic, and community leaders have little or no international education or training. Can businesses be expected to export when virtually none of their executives has had the training necessary for global vision and international competitiveness? Can elected officials be expected to understand the impact of local policy decisions on international economic development or business competitiveness when few have insight into the implications of those decisions? Can students appreciate the importance of the emerging global economy when teachers, principals, superintendents, academic deans, and college presidents and boards have not been educated about the impact of international economic and political forces and are not aware of resources available to them for seeking opportunities related to international trade.

Roles for the Community College

Few community colleges can earn their title and ignore the need to provide at least part of the solution to the problems associated with a lack of knowledge about international relations. Much is being written about how to internationalize the curricula and to require more language study and geography (O'Banion, 1989). Programs are available for exchanging faculty and students so that those who desire international experience can have it almost for the asking. Less information is available, however, concerning opportunities for assisting local (small- and medium-sized) corporations, which account for a majority of employment sources in some community college districts. While some of these executives have had limited export success through specialization in well-defined product or service niches, most have little knowledge of the international marketplace or its competitive features. Their business strategy is to look at the domestic market and then consider the global market, rather than to examine the global market as encompassing many domestic markets. The problem is that barriers to entering the worldwide marketplace are self-imposed as a result of a lack of international education and experience.

While the local community college might not be able to staff an institute for international education, it can identify the resources available in the community on which a continuing education program can be built. In each region of the country, there are individuals who have expertise that could be shared to everyone's advantage. In many situations, the problem faced by one firm has been solved by another nearby. The community college can serve as a catalyst to form a network of executives who are interested in the global marketplace. Most business people are eager to share their experiences and to learn how their peers operate in these uncharted waters. These efforts at information exchange should be concentrated on those in leadership positions since these are the individuals who can most effectively bring about change.

While the college should initiate the formation of the network and offer programs, it must build its credibility by securing the sponsorship of the corporations involved. The executives participating must identify with the programs to the point where they are willing to financially support the project. The college must recruit an advisory board composed of chief executive officers willing to devote time and resources to the cause of international education.

A second task of the community college is to provide nuts-and-bolts training to the individuals in each firm who deal with day-to-day export operations. This training is best achieved in cooperation with the state office of economic development and the U.S. Department of Commerce, other colleges and universities, and selected companies (both foreign and domestic) located in the service area. In each region there are several firms engaged in international trade. These are valuable resources that not only can be used in the development of training programs but also can act as a network of credible voices in attracting those executives who may be initially skeptical about the prospect of international business. Once the firms that are interested in world trade have been identified, the decision makers can be invited to attend seminars in which management, marketing, and cross-cultural issues that must be fully understood and resolved prior to initiating or expanding international business activity are discussed (for example, the overseas market evaluation process and market research, the internal corporate structure needed for international success, and how to find and evaluate agents and distributors).

Once the chief executive officer has decided to venture into the international marketplace, the sales and marketing decision makers of the corporation must learn about the representation agreement laws of the country or countries to be approached since each country protects its own business people. Training in how to prepare written trading agreements can prevent catastrophes later, as attested by the many disaster stories in the export arena (Crupi and Gell, 1989, p. 4).

Individuals responsible for international financing and credit decisions must understand the various methods of international payment available to firms. The proper use of letters of credit to avoid payment problems in the export process can make the difference between success or failure. There are many aspects of export financing and many different methods of identifying and managing foreign risk. Executives must understand international cash management, export factoring, and acceptance financing prior to venturing into the export business.

Shipment of a product within a state or region or even across the country is quite different from shipment across international boundaries. Someone in each firm must become familiar with the myriad forms related to each mode of shipment. International trade has its own vocabulary of terms of sale, each with its unique legal meaning for title transfer and insurance coverage. There is no one place where a firm or individual interested in entering the international marketplace can learn all of these aspects of the market. O'Banion's (1987) *Resource Handbook for International Business* was developed by Loop College and the Chicago business community in response to the business leaders' stated needs. It provides a directory of resources "to assist in expansion of international trade" (Gleazer, 1989, p. 145). The book can meet "the basic information needs of those trying to identify new export or import markets, analyze their competition, ship or clear goods, or increase profitability through creative use of export finance programs" (Gleazer, 1989, p. 145).

Conclusion

The possibility exists that somewhere in a community college's service area parts of an international trade program are in place. However, even in states where such programs are available on a statewide basis, only a small fraction of firms become involved initially. Maryland, for example, "has the most extensive international program in the country. In 1986, it appropriated $1.4 million for its international activities and employed a full-time staff of eighteen. Only nine states have appropriated more funds than Maryland and only eight states have allocated more staff to their international departments. . . . Maryland is relying heavily on port expansion in Baltimore, while Kentucky is promoting agricultural products by the creation of an export trading company. Washington and Oregon are initiating aggressive international marketing programs and California's dominance is in attracting foreign investments" (Luke, Ventriss, Reed, and Reed, 1988,

p. 132). There are market needs that should be cultivated. Given the changes in today's global economy, community college presidents can, should, and must provide the leadership necessary to proactively internationalize their collective approach to their service areas.

References

Crupi, J. A., and Gell, R. L. Becoming an International Competitor: Maryland's Strategy for the Development of the World Trade Center Institute. Dallas, Tex.: International Leadership Center, 1989.
Gleazer, E. J. "Initiatives in International Education." In T. O'Banion (ed.), Innovation in the Community College. New York: American Council on Education/Macmillan, 1989. 294 pp. (ED 305 981)
Kline, J. M. "The International Economies of U.S. States." Publius, 1984, 14 (4), 81–94.
Luke, J. S., Ventriss, C., Reed, B. J., and Reed, C. M. Managing Economic Development: A Guide to State and Local Leadership Strategies. San Francisco: Jossey-Bass, 1988.
National Governors' Association. Jobs, Growth, and Competitiveness: Productive People, Productive Policies. Washington, D.C.: National Governors' Association, 1987. 107 pp. (ED 290 350)
O'Banion, T. Resource Handbook for International Business. (2nd ed.) Chicago: Loop College, 1987.

Robert L. Gell is president of Cecil Community College in North East, Maryland, and was on assignment to the International Division of the Maryland Department of Economic and Employment Development in Baltimore from June through November 1989.

James A. Crupi is president of Strategic Leadership Solutions, Inc., located in Plano, Texas. He wrote the plan for the development of the World Trade Center Institute in Maryland.

Evaluation results can be used to demonstrate the cost-benefits of economic and work force development programs to campus and community groups.

Evaluating Results of Economic and Work Force Development Programs

Richard L. Alfred

A restructuring of the labor market is one paramount attribute of a society undergoing economic transformation. Although this task is accomplished in many ways, the preparation of a new or retrained labor force is fundamental. Community colleges have long maintained a reputation for offering low-cost career and technical training programs that produce workers with market-ready skills. They have become an ideal economic development partner for business, industry, and government.

This chapter addresses the issue of evaluating results of these economic development efforts. Although community colleges are products of the communities that they serve, the economic development role demands a different type of relationship with public- and private-sector agencies. It includes intricate linkages among agencies with similar, but not always compatible, interests. These linkages could disrupt the traditional mechanism of academic governance if not carefully developed and understood by campus groups. Therefore, evaluation results can potentially serve a dual purpose.

First, they can be used to demonstrate the obvious—how well the institution is achieving specific goals related to economic and work force development (Alfred, 1982; Alfred, 1983). How many workers are trained or retrained through programs and courses? What are the benefits experienced by workers in terms of job placement, salary, promotion, and job mobility? What is the level of employer satisfaction with the program?

Second, evaluation results can be used to demonstrate the cost-benefits of economic and work force development to campus and community constituencies. What did employers gain through participation in the program? What are the costs and benefits for state government in terms of attraction of new industry, retention of existing industry, reduction of unemployment, taxation, and so forth? What is the impact of these programs on faculty, particularly on their role in academic governance?

Context for Evaluation

It is important to understand the context in which evaluation takes place as a necessary first step in evaluating results. Indeed, far from being an abstraction, the context for economic development programs consists of serious challenges and opportunities in the external environment that affect management and governance inside the institution.

External Environment. Community colleges must now earn their way in an increasingly demanding, consumer-driven society. They have no monopoly as the providers of training and job skills required of workers to survive in the emerging global economy. Students are older and more discerning, and they choose their providers of education and training on the basis of convenience, cost, and performance in demonstrating real outcomes. Business and industry invest in training and retraining using the same bottom-line analysis of outcomes. Community colleges must change and respond to this challenge or else be relegated a limited mandate, such as basic skills and job entry, or simply be seen as irrelevant and lose public support (Gordon, 1989).

College Management and Governance. Increased economic competitiveness also represents an enormous opportunity for community colleges to demonstrate the quality of their programs when they can do so in quantifiable terms. As business and government agencies conclude that the increases in productivity required to compete internationally can only be gained by massive investment in work force training, community colleges stand to benefit from that investment. However, community colleges must change the ways that they design and develop curricula, utilize faculty, and evaluate results to take advantage of this opportunity.

Gordon (1989) has described the task ahead as follows:

> Curricula must be updated to be responsive to changing economic conditions. Faculty must remain current in their fields or adapt to new roles. Effective instructional practices need to be identified and implemented, including widespread use of instructional technology. Above all, student outcomes must be demonstrated by such measures as retention and completion rates, placement rates, student and employer satisfaction, quantifiable increases in knowledge and skills, and educational and career growth [p. 1].

In theory, community colleges are flexible institutions organized to respond quickly to economic development needs. The problem with this portrait is that community colleges cannot be viewed as altogether rational institutions. The interests pursued by faculty and administrators in relationship to economic development may not necessarily reflect common goals or center exclusively on the satisfaction of business and industry needs. Moreover, community colleges are not organized to conduct ongoing, systematic assessment of their performance in satisfying student and employer needs. The research function is poorly conceptualized, diffused among departments and divisions, and of limited utility in high-level decisions concerning programs and services. The basic resources needed to evaluate the results of economic development are at best questionable and in some colleges missing altogether.

Practical Realities Guiding Evaluation

Fundamental to the concept of economic development is the notion that the knowledge and skills produced by community colleges will satisfy the context-specific training needs of business and industry employers. As specific groups develop a stake in the economic development activities of an institution, they become a force in evaluation.

Table 11.1 lists various groups with an interest in economic development and possible motives for their interest. In this table, campus groups (faculty, students, administrators, and trustees) and extra-campus groups (workers, business/industry employers, labor unions, government agency officials, elected officials, and community interest groups) are portrayed as coalitions holding specific interests that color their needs for economic development and, ultimately, their perceptions about college programs.

Although economic development programming is a seemingly natural role for community colleges, perspectives on this role vary. For elected officials and politicians concerned about the well-being of a state or locality, economic development may be viewed as an obligation. When community colleges offer programs that train or retrain workers, attract new industry, and convert unemployed adults into tax-paying citizens, the colleges are contributors to the economy. Business and industry employers may have a different outlook. For them, the successful community college is one that consistently prepares workers with market-relevant skills at a reasonable cost in the shortest amount of time. Community college faculty and administrators represent yet another perspective. Faculty see economic development as an important role for community colleges as long as it does not interfere with academic governance or compromise the curriculum. Administrators see this role as a political necessity if community colleges are to develop public support and to acquire incremental resources.

Measurement of success in economic development programming depends on three categories of information: (1) constituency needs and expectations for economic development, (2) program design and outcomes,

**Table 11.1. Constituencies Involved in
Economic Development Programs**

Constituency	Motives for Involvement
Campus Groups	
Faculty	Expansion of resources/maintenance of standards for curriculum and instruction
Students	Cooperative education programs, upgrading job skills
Administrators	Expansion of enrollment and resources/establishment of industry linkages
Trustees	Improvement of linkages with public- and private-sector organizations in the community
Extra-Campus Groups	
Workers	Upgrading job skills needed for mobility
Business/industry employers	Upgrading of worker skills at all levels in the organization to improve productivity and quality
Labor unions	Job security for union members, full employment, upgrading job skills
Government agency officials	Training/retraining of the labor force to lower unemployment, attract and retain industry, and improve revenue
Elected officials	Establishment of industry/education linkages to attract/retain industry, lower unemployment, and improve the quality of life
Community interest groups	Attraction/retention of industry and workers to improve the economy of the local service region

and (3) constituency perceptions of program outcomes. To examine success, community colleges must collect information about results in the second and third categories and relate it to the information in the first category. In this way, practical realities that underlie the evaluation process are addressed, and a context is provided for the interpretation of results.

Designing an Evaluation Program

Before designing a program for evaluating results, it may be useful to outline the purposes to which evaluation results can be applied. (1) At the very least, evaluation results provide basic information for administrative decisions in many areas. Program development, resource allocation, and instructional delivery are a few obvious areas of use. (2) The availability of information on the outcomes of economic development programs (job training and retraining, for example) can help groups that are considering linkages with community colleges. (3) Evaluation information constitutes an important resource for institutional lobbying and public relations efforts to build a favorable image with important constituencies (for example, government agencies, elected officials, business/industry employers, labor unions, and workers).

Although individual institutional goals and service region conditions determine the exact design for evaluating results, certain information is so crucial to effective evaluation that it forms what may be called the *basic evaluation program*. The performance of the institution in producing outcomes through economic development programs that meet identified needs is at the heart of the evaluation program. As depicted in Table 11.2, the evaluation program should include several components: (1) a statement of institutional activities in economic development along with performance indicators, (2) the constituencies that benefit directly or indirectly from economic development activities, and (3) the time frame in which results should be measured. Other types of information also may be included in the basic evaluation program, depending on institutional need.

The only effective way to ensure that an evaluation program will meet present and future needs is to plan and design it carefully. The following steps, based on an organizing framework developed by Kay Maves, are crucial to successful planning (Maves, 1988, pp. 18-19). These steps are the basis of the evaluation program outlined in Table 11.2.

Step 1: Secure Institutional Commitment. If top institutional officers are not already convinced of the importance of an effective program for evaluating economic development results, they must be persuaded. Remember that economic development programs are a relatively new mission-related activity for community colleges, and that the uses of evaluation data may need to be demonstrated. A useful strategy is to present administrators with examples of the uses to which other institutions have put their economic development results. Include cases demonstrating the importance of an effective program to institutional efforts such as building new linkages with industry, lobbying state officials for resources, and marketing programs to adult learners.

Step 2: Identify Economic Development Goals and Objectives. Those responsible for evaluation must have a framework against which to measure institutional performance in economic development. Carefully stated goals and objectives should guide the selection of evaluation indicators and communicate priorities in the collection of data. They should indicate which economic development activities are most important to the institution, what constituencies are involved, what data need to be collected, and the timetable for data collection. Some indicators of performance are less important than others and, depending on college goals and priorities, can be measured less often.

Step 3: Organize Evaluation Activities. The range of possible outcomes relating to economic development needs to be considered at an early stage in

Table 11.2. Dimensions of Evaluation for Economic Development

Outcome Dimension/ Indicators	Constituency							Time Frame			
								Continuous		Periodic	
	Faculty/ Staff	Students/ Workers	Business/ Industry Employers	Government Agencies	Elected Officials	Labor Unions	Community Interest Groups	Annual	Biannual	Near-Term (1–3 Years)	Long-Term (3+ Years)
Worker Training/Mobility											
Programs, services, courses, activities offered by colleges in response to identified worker training/retraining needs	o	o	p	s	s	p	s	o			
Job attainment/retention		o	o	s	s	p		o			
Job title/classification		o	o	s	s	p		o			
Job promotion (within company)		o	o	s	s			o			
Job mobility (between companies)		o	o	s	s			o			
Relationship of job to curriculum		o	p	s	s			o			
Beginning salary/current salary		o	o	s	s			o			
Supervisory responsibility		o	o	s	s			o			

Number of workers enrolled/completing programs and courses	o	o	p	p	p	s	o
Worker satisfaction with courses	o		p	s	s	s	o
Employer satisfaction with courses	p	o	p	p	s	s	o
Economic Impact							
Rate of employment/unemployment in college service region		o	o	p	p	p	o
Spending patterns of workers in local community	o		p	p	s	p	

Note:
o = Status (of each constituency as a provider of information)
p = Primary target (for evaluation information provided by the college)
s = Secondary target (for evaluation information provided by the college)

Table 11.2. (continued)

Outcome Dimension/ Indicators	Faculty/ Staff	Students/ Workers	Business/ Industry Employers	Government Agencies	Elected Officials	Labor Unions	Community Interest Groups	Annual	Biannual	Near-Term (1–3 Years)	Long-Term (3+ Years)
Economic Impact (continued)											
Tax revenue based on property ownership and spending patterns				o	p		p				o
Gains in local economy (housing, business, investment, sales, etc.)				o	p		p				o
Attraction/Retention of Industry											
Number of existing business establishments retained/ lost in college service region	s		o	p	s				o		
Number of new business establishments attracted to college service region	s		o	p	s			o			
Additional jobs created		p	o	o	p	p	s				
Additional workers employed		p	o	o	p	p	s				

Employer Satisfaction

Number of workers per industry participating in college operated training programs	p	o	p	p	s	o
Employer perceptions of program quality: technical skill preparation basic skills analytical skills worker ethics and work attitude interpersonal skills miscellaneous skills	p	o	p	p	s	o
Willingness of employers to train additional employees in program	p	o	p	p	p	o

Note:

o = Status (of each constituency as a provider of information)
p = Primary target (for evaluation information provided by the college)
s = Secondary target (for evaluation information provided by the college)

Table 11.2. (continued)

Outcome Dimension/ Indicators	Constituency							Time Frame			
								Continuous		Periodic	
	Faculty/ Staff	Students/ Workers	Business/ Industry Employers	Government Agencies	Elected Officials	Labor Unions	Community Interest Groups	Annual	Biannual	Near-Term (1–3 Years)	Long-Term (3+ Years)
Employer Satisfaction (continued)											
Employer perceptions of need for new and/or additional programs		p	o	p	p	p		o			
Employer recommendations for modification of program(s)	p		o					o			
College Costs/Benefits/Visibility											
Costs associated with economic development programs	o		p	p	p	s	s				
Direct benefits to college enrollment revenue	o		s	p	s						

Favorable/unfavorable
constituency perceptions
of college

	faculty/staff	students	business/industry	employers	government agencies	elected officials	workers	labor unions	community groups
faculty/staff	o								
students	o								
business/industry	p	p	o	p	s		p	o	
employers	p	p	o	p	s		s	o	
government agencies	p	p	p	p	s	s	s		o
elected officials	p	p	p	o	s	s			
workers	o	p	p	p	p	s			
labor unions	p	p	p	p	o		o		
community groups	p	p	p	p	o		o		

Note:
o = Status (of each constituency as a provider of information)
p = Primary target (for evaluation information provided by the college)
s = Secondary target (for evaluation information provided by the college)

the evaluation program. Table 11.2 lists five dimensions to classify the results (outcomes) that can be anticipated in most institutions: worker training/mobility, economic impact, attraction/retention of industry, employer satisfaction, and college costs/benefits/visibility. Representatives from different areas of the institution who will use the results of evaluation should participate. Apart from having needs common to all other participants, each representative will express individual needs and concerns, based on the work of his or her office, that will affect the thinking of the total group.

Step 4: Identify Constituencies. Beginning with the earliest exploratory sessions, evaluators should be thinking about the various groups involved in evaluation. These groups should be considered from two vantage points: (1) those holding evaluation information needed by the college and (2) those needing evaluation information from the college. Table 11.2 provides a list of constituencies in each category. It also indicates the status of each constituency as a provider of information (o) and as a primary (p) or secondary (s) target for evaluation information produced by the college. Different groups will be more or less important depending on the extent to which the information that they need or provide affects institutional resources.

Step 5: Select Outcome Indicators. College staff must identify the different types of information needed to evaluate the results of economic development programs. This is a pragmatic step, in which evaluators examine the spectrum of economic development activities taking place, identify the groups involved, and specify potential outcomes. The objective is to choose indicators that accurately measure college performance in meeting the economic development needs of different constituencies.

All indicators that conceivably could relate to economic development must be considered. For example, Table 11.2 lists twenty-eight outcome indicators in five categories. These indicators may be easily quantified, or they may require considerable effort. Whatever the case, the specification of outcome indicators in quantifiable form is the most important step in evaluation. It is often impossible to state each indicator in easily measured terms, but evaluators must try. At the very least, they will be able to determine the time and resources that must be devoted to evaluation.

Step 6: Assign Data Collection Priorities. Evaluators must balance cost against need, and against the availability of information, in determining priorities for data collection. Under major constraints of time and budget, evaluators may assign highest priority to easily measured outcomes with high "payoff" potential. Collection of information about workers retrained through job skills programs and about employer satisfaction with these programs provides a good example of a high-payoff project. The information can be collected in a short amount of time using standard measurement procedures, and it will yield substantial benefits to institutions seeking to build better linkages with business and industry. The time and resource requirements would be different for an evaluation activity focused on measuring the direct and indirect economic impact of economic development programs. If priorities are developed with short- and long-term benefits in mind, evaluators can begin in a relatively modest way and expand efforts as resources become available.

Step 7: Determine Measurement Methods and Time Frames. This step is crucial to current and comprehensive outcomes information. In too many instances, outcomes information is limited because evaluators have selected measurement methods and employed time frames based on convenience. Staff frequently send out close-ended questionnaires or conduct telephone interviews with a sample of workers or employers without considering more intensive measurement methods. In other cases, information is simply not collected because time and resources are insufficient to permit evaluation. The practice of selecting measurement methods and time frames based on convenience should be avoided whenever possible. Perhaps a special allocation of resources can be made to support intensive research on long-term outcomes of economic development.

Appropriate time frames for collection of evaluation data are presented in Table 11.2. For indicators measuring short-term outcomes such as worker training and retraining, a continuous assessment program is needed. A periodic assessment program is more appropriate for indicators such as the direct and indirect economic impact of economic development programs.

Step 8: Determine Report Formats and Dissemination Strategies. When the preceding steps have been completed, attention can be directed to report formats and dissemination strategies. Different designs may be required for reports having different purposes. In the case of business and industry employers, care must be taken to present information that will command the attention of busy executives and mid-level managers. The report must be short, contain meaningful information, and communicate in a language that is interesting and easily understood. The strategy for government agencies may be different. Here the emphasis could be on "bottom-line" reporting of outcomes (for example, number and locations of courses offered, number of workers trained/retrained, job skills acquired, and job mobility) that can be compared to costs. Other reports providing information about the long-term impact of economic development programs will be more extensive, although most will be conducted on a periodic basis to keep costs down.

The methods for reporting information may be modest or complex, expensive or inexpensive. At the least, community colleges should identify a "basic format" that can be used for most reports. Interviews can be conducted with representatives of agencies and organizations that receive reports to find out what type of information is desired and how it should be presented. Follow-up research can be conducted to determine the impact of this information on different groups and organizations. This follow-up should solicit feedback describing reactions to the content and style of the report(s). If the reactions are decidedly negative, changes should be made in the format to accommodate various audiences.

Applying Results to Decision Making

Community college faculty and administrators with access to economic development results will have choices with respect to the uses of this information. By applying results to decisions involving program design and resources, administrators and faculty can cultivate favorable perceptions of educational programs. Likewise, staff willing to use results to support new initiatives in economic development are more likely to meet with success than are those using hearsay evidence. However, it is not an easy task to determine the extent to which institutions should use economic development results to support major decisions. A decision that satisfies one audience may not satisfy another. For example, changes in program design and delivery identified through research carried out with business and industry employers are likely to satisfy this constituency, but not necessarily the faculty members who teach the courses involved. Essentially, evaluators working with economic development results need to understand the context in which the information has been collected and the types of decisions to which the information will be applied.

It is possible to illustrate the importance of context in the application of results to decision making by examining the relationship between economic development results and constituency views of information in one outcome dimension: worker training and mobility. Business and industry employers viewing information about worker enrollment in college courses are apt to focus on the job skills obtained in making their recommendations about program change. The emphasis will be on changes in instructional strategy, course content, and delivery to produce a more highly trained worker in a shorter amount of time. Faculty looking at the same information may have a different interpretation. To them, the acquisition of certain types of knowledge, in addition to job skills, is essential. Information from the humanities and social sciences about the effects of advancing technology, working cooperatively in small groups, ethics, effective supervision, and so forth—information superfluous to employers because it stretches the period of education—is valued by faculty because it contributes to a well-rounded worker with thinking and reasoning skills. These views applied to economic development results demonstrate different ways in which information can be used in decision making. They point to a need for evaluators to carefully consider the context in which evaluation takes place and the trade-offs among constituencies before applying information to decisions.

Conclusion

Given the cost, the problems of acquiring information from multiple constituencies, and the time required to develop a sound program for evaluating economic development results, community college administrators
and faculty may well ask, is it worth it? In response, advocates of evaluation point to the consequences of inadequate information in establishing
linkages with organizations and building positive perceptions among constituencies. Effective decision making depends on good information.
Unfortunately, community colleges are not organized to collect and inter-
pret information with any degree of consistency. Resources that can be
applied to evaluation are limited and are likely to remain so. Although it
might be difficult to address all areas of economic development in need
of evaluation, assessment of basic results using simple, cost-saving procedures has credibility, and the yield will be well worth the investment.

References

Alfred, R. L. "Improving College Resources Through Impact Assessment." In R. L.
Alfred (ed.), *Institutional Impacts on Campus, Community, and Business Communi-
ties*. New Directions for Community Colleges, no. 38. San Francisco: Jossey-Bass,
1982. 130 pp. (ED 217 944)
Alfred, R. L. "Measuring the Socioeconomic Impact of a Community College." *Junior
College Resource Review*. Los Angeles: ERIC Clearinghouse for Junior Colleges,
1983.
Gordon, R. A. "Global Perspectives Required for College Leaders." *Leadership
Abstracts*, 1989, 2 (11), 1.
Maves, K. "Managing Information on Alumni." In G. S. Melchiori (ed.), *Applying
Alumni Research to Fundraising*. New Directions for Institutional Research, no. 4.
San Francisco: Jossey-Bass, 1988.

*Richard L. Alfred is associate professor of higher and adult continuing education
at the University of Michigan, Ann Arbor, and director of the Community College
Consortium: University of Michigan, University of Toledo, and Michigan State
University.*

An annotated bibliography is provided on community colleges in relation to economic development, including general background on the topic, descriptions of community college services to business, and overviews of community college participation in state and local economic development activities.

Sources and Information: Community Colleges and Economic Development

Diane Hirshberg

This volume demonstrates that community colleges have a significant role to play in state and local economic development activities. Community colleges can provide services from job training and entrepreneurial assistance to economic planning and community development. The role that colleges take in economic development can vary according to community needs as well as to the programs that colleges choose to develop.

The following source citations represent the most current literature in the ERIC database on community colleges and economic development. Most ERIC documents (references with "ED" numbers) can be read on microfiche at over eight hundred libraries worldwide. In addition, most may be ordered on microfiche or paper copy from the ERIC Document Reproduction Service (EDRS) at (800) 443-ERIC. Journal articles are not available from EDRS. Most journal articles can be acquired through regular library channels, or purchased for $11.75 per copy from UMI Articles Clearinghouse at (800) 521-0600, extension 533.

General Articles

These articles present overviews of community college involvement in economic and work force development activities nationwide, as well as ideas for further involvement of colleges in such activities.

American Association of Community and Junior Colleges. *Productive America: Two-Year Colleges Unite to Improve Productivity in the Nation's Workforce.*

Executive Summary and Reports 1 and 2. Washington, D.C.: American Association of Community and Junior Colleges, 1990. 160 pp. (ED 317 224)

The Productive American Project was initiated by the National Council for Occupational Education to explore human resource issues related to productivity and competitiveness, and the role of two-year colleges in human resource development. The results of this project are presented in two reports. The first discusses several issues related to productivity, and the second reviews current public policy issues related to the role of two-year colleges in work force productivity. Recommendations are directed toward two-year colleges and their national organizations and toward the U.S. Department of Labor.

Fifield, M. L. "Workers for the World: Occupational Programs in a Global Economy." *Community, Technical, and Junior College Journal*, 1990, *61* (1), 15-19.

This article reports on a survey conducted to determine whether two-year colleges are prepared to meet commercial and industrial needs for a more sophisticated and globally competitive work force. It presents findings related to the internationalization of occupational curricula, short-term training and services, the characteristics of heavily involved colleges, and the impetus for change.

Katsinas, S. G., and Lacey, V. A. "Community Colleges and Economic Development." *Community Services Catalyst*, 1990, *20* (1), 6-14.

An overview is provided of traditional and nontraditional approaches to community college involvement in economic development, highlighting national, state, and institutional initiatives. The authors contrast traditional (for example, long-term, on-campus degree programs) and nontraditional (for example, short-term, work-site, customized training) approaches.

Mora, P. L., and Giovannini, E. V. "Focus on the '90s: Clarifying the Role of Community Colleges in Economic Development." *Community Services Catalyst*, 1989, *19* (4), 8-14.

Mora and Giovannini review the literature and research on the role of community colleges in promoting economic and human resource development, providing occupational education, promoting community involvement in economic development, and surveying and meeting the training needs of business and industry.

Waddell, G. "Tips for Training a World-Class Work Force." *Community, Technical, and Junior College Journal*, 1990, *60* (4), 21-27.

Waddell examines trends in work force training needs and innovative approaches to meeting those needs (for example, business incubators, small business development centers, 2 + 2 programs, and cooperative education programs). She suggests ways in which community colleges can become more involved in work force development.

Services to Businesses

Community colleges can provide invaluable services to businesses through the provision of job-training services via contract training, as a source of trained workers, and through consulting arrangements that provide management and development expertise.

Brooks, A. "South Carolina's Special Schools: A Dollars and 'Sense' Incentive." *Community, Technical, and Junior College Journal,* 1990, *61* (4), 38–41.
This article describes South Carolina's program of special schools, which offer crash training through the state's two-year technical colleges to help new and expanding industries begin their operations through preemloyment training programs. The special schools' diversity in training, quick response to industry needs, and individually styled training are highlighted.

Carnevale, A. P., Gainer, L. J., Villet, J., and Holland, S. L. *Training Partnerships: Linking Employers and Providers.* Alexandria, Va.: American Society for Training and Development, 1990. 52 pp. (ED 319 925)
This overview of job-training partnerships begins by considering the formation of linkages between employers and providers as a common business transaction. It identifies services available from providers, offers guidelines for locating and selecting a provider, and discusses the evaluation of linkage relationships. Part Two describes the providers of training and identifies educational institutions. Part Three focuses on the various types of training. Part Four discusses the creation of a linkage as a learning experience.

Palmer, J. *How Do Community Colleges Serve Business and Industry? A Review of Issues Discussed in the Literature.* Washington, D.C.: American Association of Community and Junior Colleges, 1990. 62 pp. (ED 319 443)
The educational literature provides evidence of the increasing role of community colleges in serving business and industry. By providing preservice education for persons entering the labor market or continuing education for employed individuals who seek skills upgrading, community colleges have made businesses a major consumer of college services. Following an overview of community college services to business clients, Palmer examines the role of the community college in economic development and summarizes research on administrative factors. Factors that influence community college involvement with business and industry are identified.

Warford, L. J. "A Study of Customized Contract Training Programs at Selected Community Colleges." Unpublished doctoral dissertation, University of Oregon, 1989. 202 pp. Available from University Microfilms International (order no. 89-18957).

In 1987, a study was conducted to assess the status of customized contract training programs in sixteen community college districts and to examine the issues surrounding the establishment of these programs. The study found that (1) contract training programs increased dramatically over the past decade, with enrollments increasing from less than five thousand in 1980 to nearly sixty-eight thousand in 1987; (2) the majority of the institutions did not profit financially from the programs, though some believed that the programs helped fulfill the mission of the college; and (3) ideally, contract training programs are developed cooperatively by the college and the client firm. The survey instrument is appended.

Wuertele, P. "The Business and Industry Liaison as Consultant." *Community, Technical, and Junior College Journal,* 1990, *60* (4), 26-27.

Wuertele explores the nature of consulting in community college partnerships with business and industry. She considers examples of community college personnel acting in the roles of objective observers, process counselors, fact finders, alternative identifiers, links to resources, joint problem solvers, trainers, information specialists, and advocates.

Zeiss, T. "Employee Retention: A Challenge of the Nineties." *Community, Technical, and Junior College Journal,* 1990, *60* (4), 34-37.

Zeiss considers ways in which community colleges can help employers implement programs to improve the work environment and retain trained workers. He presents a model for employee retention that has worked effectively in Pueblo, Colorado. He then describes Pueblo Community College's cooperative program with the Wats Marketing Group to help reduce employee turnover.

Community Colleges and State Economic Development Activities

Community colleges can play an integral role in state economic development activities, in both planning and provision of services. The following articles offer a few examples of such involvements.

Illinois Community College Board (ICCB). *Preparation for Employment: Programs at Illinois Public Community Colleges.* Springfield, Ill.: ICCB, 1989. 17 pp. (ED 305 971)

This report highlights the involvement of Illinois public community colleges in preparing individuals for employment. After reviewing the state's community college system, the report describes the components and aspects of employment preparation, including occupational programs and services, programs to meet the training needs of industry, mechanisms to ensure quality, adult basic and secondary education and remedial instruction, partnerships with commerce and industry, cooperation with state agencies and statewide initiatives, articulation with secondary schools and industry, and funding and financial aid. The report concludes with a discussion of challenges facing the colleges in the future.

Lightfield, E. T., and others. *Challenges Toward the Year 2000: A Report of the Chancellor's Task Force on the Role of the Virginia Community College System in Economic Development.* Richmond: Virginia State Department of Community Colleges, 1989. 41 pp. (ED 312 016)

This task force report examines the future of Virginia's community colleges in economic development and work place literacy. The report sets forth ten challenges that stand as obstacles to the full realization of the state's potential for economic development and adult literacy and recommends and describes strategies for dealing with them. Underpinning the recommendations are five primary goals for the colleges: playing a proactive role in the local community; forming and advancing partnerships and collaboration with other institutions, agencies, and corporations; responding to demands for work place literacy and training; and seeking increased funding.

Starnes, P. M., and Johnson, B. E. "Educational Initiatives for Industrial Development in Georgia." Paper presented at the College Industry Education Conference of the American Society for Engineering Education, San Diego, California, February 8–12, 1988. 7 pp. (ED 306 967)

Georgia's two-year technical institutes have played a prominent role in linking education with industry. Five major interrelated efforts have worked to transform the state from an agrarian economy to one utilizing advanced technologies. First, the Quick-Start Program offers state-paid services to new or expanding industries. Second, the Advanced Technology Development Center of the Georgia Institute of Technology serves as a business incubator for new companies, reduces business risks for advanced technology companies, and links new job creation to entrepreneurial innovation. Third, a study defined directions and strategies to meet advanced technology training needs at two-year colleges and to assist technical institutes in serving new industry attracted to the state. Fourth, a standard engineering technology curriculum was created for six technical institutes to offer an associate degree in applied technology on a trial basis. Fifth, the State Board of Postsecondary Vocational Education was created to oversee engineering technology education and the role of postsecondary education in industrial development.

Community Colleges and Local Economic Development Activities

One of the areas in which community colleges can have a large impact is local economic development. Community colleges can provide job-training and community development services that are often unavailable elsewhere and can respond to the specific needs of local industry.

Blong, J. T., and Shultz, R. M. "The Dislocated Worker: When Training Is Not Enough." *Community, Technical, and Junior College Journal,* 1990, *60* (4), 28-32.

In this article, the authors discuss the socioeconomic effects of plant closures, focusing on the problems faced by dislocated workers who lack the financial resources to complete a retraining program. They describe the Eastern Iowa Community College District's efforts to train and counsel dislocated workers through its Caterpillar Worker Assistance Center.

Mellander, G. A., and Prochaska, F. *Accessing Resources Through Consortium Arrangements.* Saratoga, Calif.: West Valley-Mission Community College District, 1990. 58 pp. (ED 318 493)

In an effort to pool resources and funds, West Valley-Mission Community College District (WVMCCD) has found the consortia approach to developing new programs and services efficient and effective. Employer-based training programs, drug abuse education, articulation agreements, apprenticeship programs, and economic development programs are a few of the activities that have been successfully accomplished through consortia efforts at WVMCCD. These partnership programs encourage the pooling of resources and can reduce duplication of effort and afford participants a superior chance to receive funding in a competitive situation. This source offers guidelines for consortium development.

Parees, B., and Bartok, L. A. "Jobs for Economic Growth: An Allegheny County Joint Initiative Project." *Community Services Catalyst,* 1989, *19* (4), 27-28.

This article describes the Community College of Allegheny County's Jobs for Economic Growth Project, which provides county residents with paid public-service work experience, vocational training at the work site, educational opportunities outside of work time, and support services. It highlights program components, including assessment, individual program planning, and job search assistance.

Thomas, M. G. *A Portfolio of Community College Initiatives in Rural Economic Development.* Kansas City, Mo.: Midwest Research Institute, 1989. 124 pp. (ED 310 901)

Community colleges across the United States have initiated programs that are making an impact on the productivity of rural America and its residents. This report profiles twenty community and technical college initiatives in rural economic development, including diverse approaches for training rural cottage-industry operators, grants for community organizers, grower cooperatives, rural diversified enterprise centers, venture capital networks, advanced manufacturing demonstrations, government procurement programs, economic development classes, and work place literacy programs.

Diane Hirshberg is user services coordinator at the ERIC Clearinghouse for Junior Colleges, University of California, Los Angeles.

INDEX

Abili, K., 75, 76
Abreu, F. J., 74, 76
Accreditation, in health care, 57
Active Corps of Executives, 28
Alfred, R. L., 85, 99
Allen D. N., 31n, 33, 38
American Association of Community and Junior Colleges, 11, 15, 20, 23, 31, 38, 51, 53, 101–102; international membership in, 70, 76
American Association of State Colleges and Universities, 47, 53
American Nurses' Association, 59
American Society for Training and Development, 3
Andrade, A. F., 74, 76
Arizona, small business assistance program of, 9, 15
Aslanian, C. B., 10, 12, 15, 26, 30
Austria, community college concept in, 72-73, 76

Bartok, L. A., 106
Bay Area Council, 14
Bay State Skills Corporation, 22
Bazan, E. J., 33, 38
Ben Franklin Partnership, 45
Betz, F., 10, 12, 15, 26, 30
Birch, D., 32, 38
Blong, J. T., 106
Bogart, Q. J., 73, 76
Brawer, F. B., 69, 77
Brazil, community college concept in, 70, 73-75, 76
Breagy, J., 31n
Breneman, D. W., 19, 23
Breuder, R. L., 22, 23
Brey, R., 64, 68
Brooks, A., 103
Burnier, D., 31, 39
Burrows, W. R., 57, 61
Business incubators, 4, 31, 102. See also Rural business incubators
Buss, T. F., 32, 33, 38

California: Employment Training Panel program of, 21; industry/community college cooperation in, 13–14, 15; trade program of, 83
Campbell, C., 33, 38
Canada, community college concept in, 70-72
Capital. See Human capital; Physical capital
Carmichael, J. B., 25, 30
Carnevale, A. P., 3, 5, 19, 23, 48, 49, 52, 53, 103
Carter, D. J., 69, 77
Castro, C. M., 74, 77
Caterpillar Worker Assistance Center, 106
Charner, I., 22, 23
Chmura, T. J., 7, 15
Circle West, regional incubation system of, 34, 36-37
Coates, J. F., 3, 5
Cohen, A. M., 69, 77
Collaboration, in North Carolina, 12–13
Committee on Allied Health Education and Accreditation, 57
Committee for Economic Development, 7, 15
Community College of Allegheny County, 106
Community college concept, 69, 76; in Brazil, 70, 73-75, 76; in Canada, 70-72; export of, 69-70; in Germany/Austria, 72-73; in Iran, 75-76
Community colleges: and cooperative education programs, 49, 50-53; economic development partnership programs of, 8-14; and evaluation of programs, 85-99; and global economy, 81-84; health care training at, 60-61; and human capital, 17-18, 22-23; leadership of presidents of, 41-46; literature on, and economic development, 101-107; 1980s experimentation at, 7-8; 1990s direction of, 14-15; and physical capital, 22, 23; recommendations for, on work force development, 3-4; and rural business incubation, 34-38; and SBDCs, 26-30, 31; telecourses of, 63-68; training of nurses at, 58, 59; and work force crisis, 48

leges, 81-84; in global economy, 79-81; and Montgomery Community College, 30

Iowa, Industrial New Jobs Training program of, 21

Iran, community college concept in, 75-76

Japan, community college concept in, 70, 76

Jarratt, J., 3, 5

Jobs Inc., 36

Job-training partnerships, 103

Johnson, B. E., 105

Johnston, W. B., 18, 20, 23, 48, 53

Jones, E. B., 70, 77

Junior colleges, in Japan, 70, 76

Katsinas, S. G., 43, 46, 102

Kempner, K., 73, 74, 77

Kentucky, trade program of, 83

Kiamichi Area Vocational Technical Schools System (KAVTS), incubator of, 36

Kintzer, F. C., 70, 75, 77

Kline, J. M., 80, 84

Kopecek, R. J., 41, 46

Labette Community College (Parsons, Kansas), incubator at, 34-36

Lacey, V. A., 43, 46, 102

LaGuardia Community College (Long Island, New York), co-op program of, 51

Lane Community College (Eugene, Oregon), 8, 28

Leadership, of community college presidents, 41-46

Learning, and healthy economy, 3

Lehigh Valley Partnership, 45

Levin, J. S., 71, 72, 77

Lightfield, E. T., 105

Livieratos, B. B., 64, 68

Loop College, 83

Lorain County Community College, technology training at, 11

Luke, J. S., 80, 83, 84

MacDougall, P. R., 43, 44, 46

McNett, I., 9, 11, 13, 15

Magruder, D. R., 21, 23

Mahaffie, J. B., 3, 5

Malecki, E. J., 33, 38

Maricopa Community College District (Phoenix, Arizona), 9

Maryland: nursing education model of, 56; Partnership Through Workforce Quality program of, 21-22; technology transfer program in, 22; trade program of, 83

Maryland, University of, 22

Massachusetts, Bay State Skills Corporation program of, 22

Maves, K., 89, 99

Mellander, G. A., 106

Melville, J. G., 7, 15

Mercer County Community College (Trenton, New Jersey), 28-29

Miller, L. W., 63, 68

Mitre Corporation, 49

Montgomery Community College, 29-30; survey at, 65-67

Montgomery, J., 34, 35, 37, 38

Mora, P. L., 102

Morgan, J., 34, 35, 37, 38

Myers, J., 34, 35, 37, 38

National Business Incubation Association (NBIA), 34, 38

National Council for Occupational Education, 102

National Governors' Association, 7, 15, 19, 21, 24, 80, 81, 84

Nelson, S. C., 19, 23

Nespoli, L. A., 17, 24

New federalism, 17

Newman, F., 19, 24

North Arkansas Community College System (Salem, Arkansas), 34

North Carolina, collaboration in, 12-13, 15

Northern Virginia Community College (NOVA) (Alexandria, Virginia), 49; co-op program of, 51, 52

Nursing: education programs in, 58-60; new jobs in, 55

O'Banion, T., 4, 5, 81, 83, 84

Ohio: technology training in, 11, 14-15; technology transfer in, 22

Ohio State University, 11, 22

Ohio Technology Transfer Organization, 11, 22

Oregon: Small Business Development Centers in, 8-9, 14-15; trade program of, 83

Organizations, and economic development programs, 13-14

Ordering Information

New Directions for Community Colleges is a series of paperback books that provides expert assistance to help community colleges meet the challenges of their distinctive and expanding educational mission. Books in the series are published quarterly in Fall, Winter, Spring, and Summer and are available for purchase by subscription as well as by single copy.

Subscriptions for 1991 cost $48.00 for individuals (a savings of 20 percent over single-copy prices) and $70.00 for institutions, agencies, and libraries. Please do not send institutional checks for personal subscriptions. Standing orders are accepted.

Single copies cost $15.95 when payment accompanies order. (California, New Jersey, New York, and Washington, D.C., residents please include appropriate sales tax.) Billed orders will be charged postage and handling.

Discounts for quantity orders are available. Please write to the address below for information.

All orders must include either the name of an individual or an official purchase order number. Please submit your order as follows:
Subscriptions: specify series and year subscription is to begin
Single copies: include individual title code (such as CC1)

Mail all orders to:
Jossey-Bass Inc., Publishers
350 Sansome Street
San Francisco, California 94104

For sales outside of the United States contact:
Maxwell Macmillan International Publishing Group
866 Third Avenue
New York, New York 10022

OTHER TITLES AVAILABLE IN THE
NEW DIRECTIONS FOR COMMUNITY COLLEGES SERIES
Arthur M. Cohen, Editor-in-Chief
Florence B. Brawer, Associate Editor